Jaume Plensa. The Four Elements

Our body is the home of the spirit. The place in which ideas live. Our body is a meeting place where our different experiences converge, mix and grow, creating a colossal archive. The University is an extension of our body. A gathering space in which people and ideas, traditions and future, meet to converse, weaving the mesh of human knowledge.

—Jaume Plensa

JAUME PLENSA
THE FOUR ELEMENTS

Edited by Geert Bouckaert

LEUVEN UNIVERSITY PRESS

Table of Contents

The four elements
Sint Raphäel

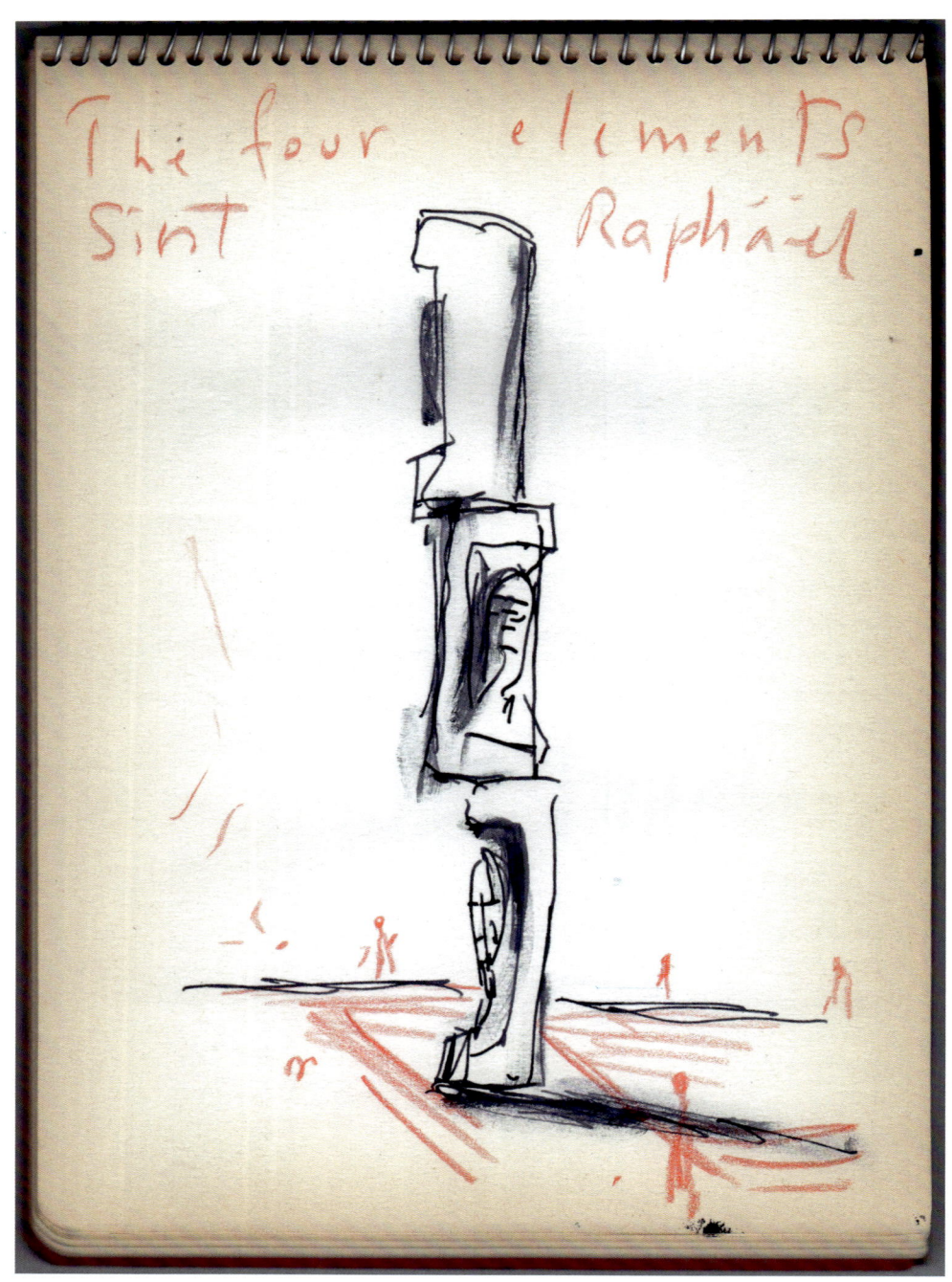

A Proper Tribute

How can we pay proper tribute to the donors of Opening the future? With that initial question, Professor Geert Bouckaert and I sat around the table with Rector Luc Sels. During that brainstorming session, the idea arose to bring to Leuven a work of art by the famous Catalan artist Jaume Plensa. His piece *Body of Knowledge* was very reminiscent of the 'knowledge of the body' and 'knowledge of the brain' that Opening the future is all about.

Opening the future is KU Leuven's major giving initiative, one that has grown into a warm community of committed donor families, passionate researchers, and the university's visionary leadership. As chair, I am immensely proud that we have built this circle of patronage around the university. The mission of Opening the future is clear: to find solutions to dementia and cancer by providing a major financial boost to excellent scientific research.

Excellence has been characteristic of KU Leuven for 600 years. This historic anniversary provides the ideal opportunity to thank the many patrons who together have lent their support to research and teaching at my alma mater. Is there a better place to pay tribute to those donors than the University Library, just about the most famous gift the university was ever privileged to receive? The sculpture in the gallery is called *Fire* and commemorates the resurrection of the library after the devastating fire in World War I. It testifies to the strength of people when they stand together in support of a cause, as does Opening the future.

From Ladeuze Square, it is barely a kilometer as the crow flies to the second part of this artwork, *Water, Earth, Air* which rises like a totem pole on the Hertogen site, the new crossroads of health care and medicine. Not coincidentally, this site is halfway between the University Library and UZ Leuven, and *Water, Earth, Air* forms the connecting link between the city and medicine.

Plensa's works are iconic and stand in some of the most evocative places in the world. Leuven now stands prominently on that list. What touches me most in Plensa's sculptures is that they are monumental and subdued at the same time, which we also see here in *The Four Elements*. The heads have their eyes closed, and I wonder what they are dreaming or thinking. They show the vulnerable human being who is simultaneously capable of so much. The sturdy bronze design is firmly grounded, while eliciting an almost ethereal feeling. The sculptures leave no one unmoved and constantly interact with the viewer, prompting thought and profound feeling. I associate this interaction between body and mind, the earthly and the cerebral, with Opening the future.

Those suffering from dementia struggle with a faltering memory, an inability to find language, a blurring of the line between delusion and truth. The once mighty brain sputters and fails, much to the distress of patients and those around them. It makes us realize that in the end we, too, are 'only' a body, made of stardust, evolved from fire, earth, water, and air.

And yet. We count on our brilliant researchers to fathom our brain and find the cure that can deliver us from neurodegeneration. The answer can only come from science, which searches and considers, whirls and analyzes, studies and concludes. With the financial support of donors, researchers can freely tread unknown paths. For it is along those paths that breakthroughs can be found. And so the circle is complete. A work of art as a poetic expression of man's great (in)ability, as well as a memento of the power of collaboration.

Finally, a warm word of thanks to the donors of Opening the future and our excellent researchers. Thanks also to KU Leuven and Rector Luc Sels. Thank you to Professor Geert Bouckaert. Thank you to the City of Leuven and Mayor Mohamed Ridouani. Our shared drive and ambition brought this feat to fruition. And last but not least, thanks to Jaume Plensa for this wonderful creation.

Urbain Vandeurzen
Chair of KU Leuven's Opening the future and Entrepreneur-Maecenas

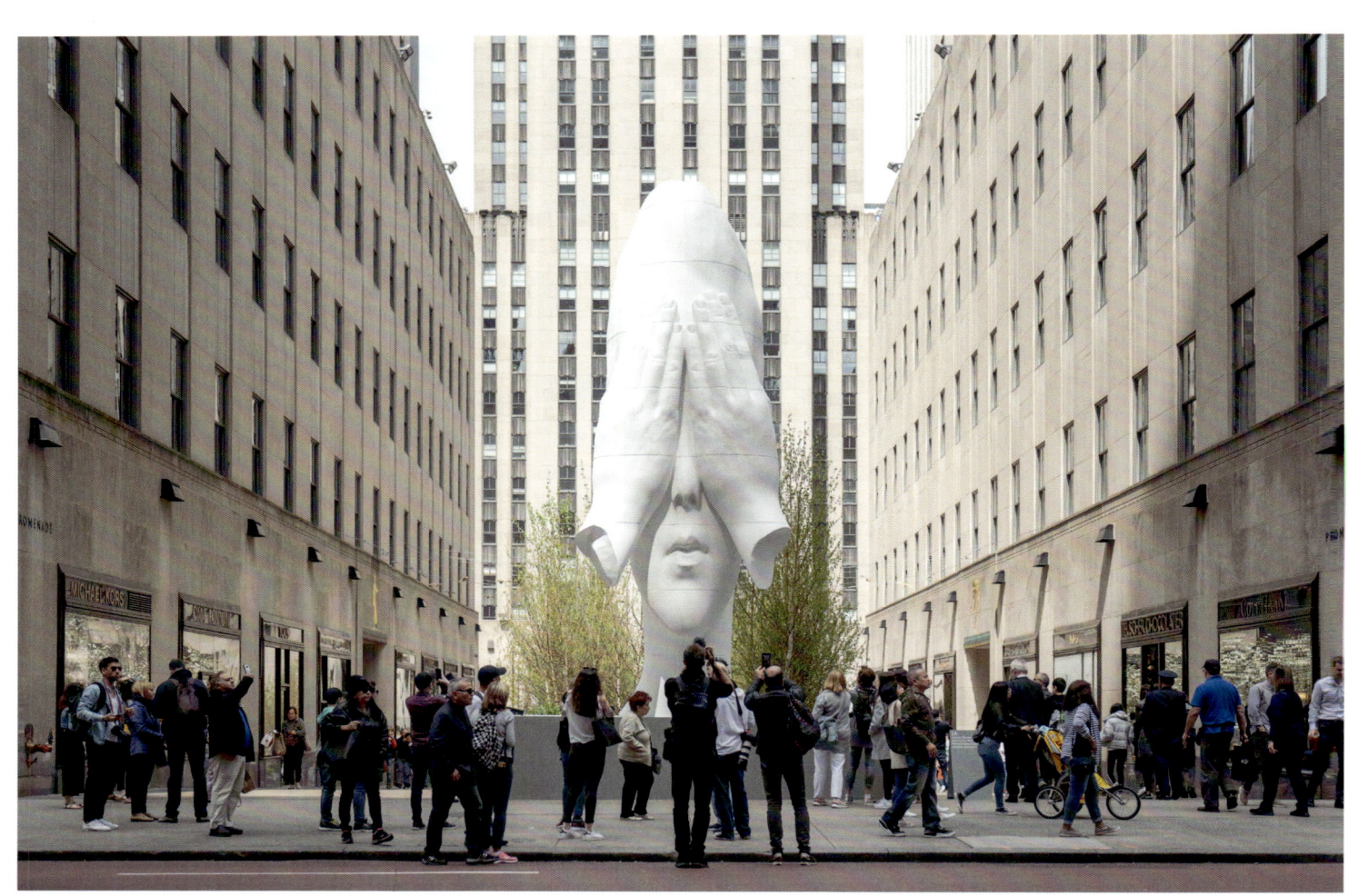

Knowledge and Art

The university is a place where knowledge and art interact, ever since the beginning of universities, so many centuries ago. Challenging scholars and students to think critically about the world around them, contemporary art plays an important role in this interaction, as it pushes the boundaries of traditional forms and practices, and explores new ways of expression and creativity. Knowledge and imagination, research and creativity, are two ways to orient ourselves, two ways towards a more encompassing attitude.

At the university, scholars and students are encouraged to find and express their own voices and develop their own perspectives. Contemporary art offers them an opportunity to do so through various mediums such as painting, sculpture, performance art, and new media. In addition, contemporary art is often a mirror of society as well as a platform for discussion on current issues such as politics, identity, technology, and the environment. By studying and creating art, by experiencing and being challenged, a university community learns to think critically and reflect on their own position in the world.

The university is therefore fertile ground for the creation of innovative and inspiring works of art. By collaborating with artists and curators, a university can and should broaden its horizons and explore new artistic avenues.

In short, university and contemporary art combine to create a dynamic and fertile ground that challenges all its members to grow and flourish as creative thinkers and makers. It is a place where art and knowledge come together and where the imagination is given free rein.

In this respect, it is truly an honor and a privilege to welcome Jaume Plensa to KU Leuven. His artistic work represents in a most excellent way this connection between art and science, between imagination and knowledge. Along with the Massachusetts Institute of Technology, Leuven considers itself happy and enthusiastic alike to create a home for Plensa's new opus in our city. Standing in a long tradition, and referring explicitly to the famous sculptures by Henry Moore, Jaume Plensa innovates and renews this tradition. In his own words: "Sculpture is not only talking about volumes. It is talking about something deep inside ourselves that without sculpture we cannot describe." He explains, "We are always with one foot in normal life and one foot in the most amazing abstraction. And that is the contradiction, that is life." In this ongoing search, Jaume Plensa brings us back to the very origins of culture and society, to that which goes beyond ages and centuries and becomes eternal and sacred. The four elements in Plensa's work were exactly what the first Greek philosophers coined as the *archè*, the first principle, what is at the beginning and what remains ever after.

Fire, earth, air, and water are the themes in Jaume Plensa's creation for Leuven. It consists of two sculptures. In the University Library on Ladeuze Square, *Fire* has been given a place; on St. Raphaël's Square, next to the future Vesalius Museum, three other elements have been stacked on top of each other like a totem: *Water*, *Earth*, and *Air*. Jaume Plensa's work shows the connection between university and city, between science and art, between care and institutions. The four elements – fire, water, earth, and air – create man, says the university. The four faces look together in different directions.

Most obviously, *Fire* at the library relates immediately to the history of this place. Leuven University Library was destroyed by fire in 1914. Solidarity extended worldwide at the time and help came from all corners.

Jaume Plensa's sculptures, sometimes monumental but always humanistic, have left their mark on all five continents of our world, and the way he uses urban space has left its mark on people's minds. Wherever they are installed, the works of this artist radiate a special energy, not only by their presence in space but also by the way the artist works with materials.

By installing Jaume Plensa's *Water*, *Earth, Air* and *Fire,* KU Leuven is proud to enrich its growing collection of contemporary art. In this way, Plensa's creations are a most welcome encouragement to make our collection accessible to a larger audience.

Luc Sels
Rector of KU Leuven

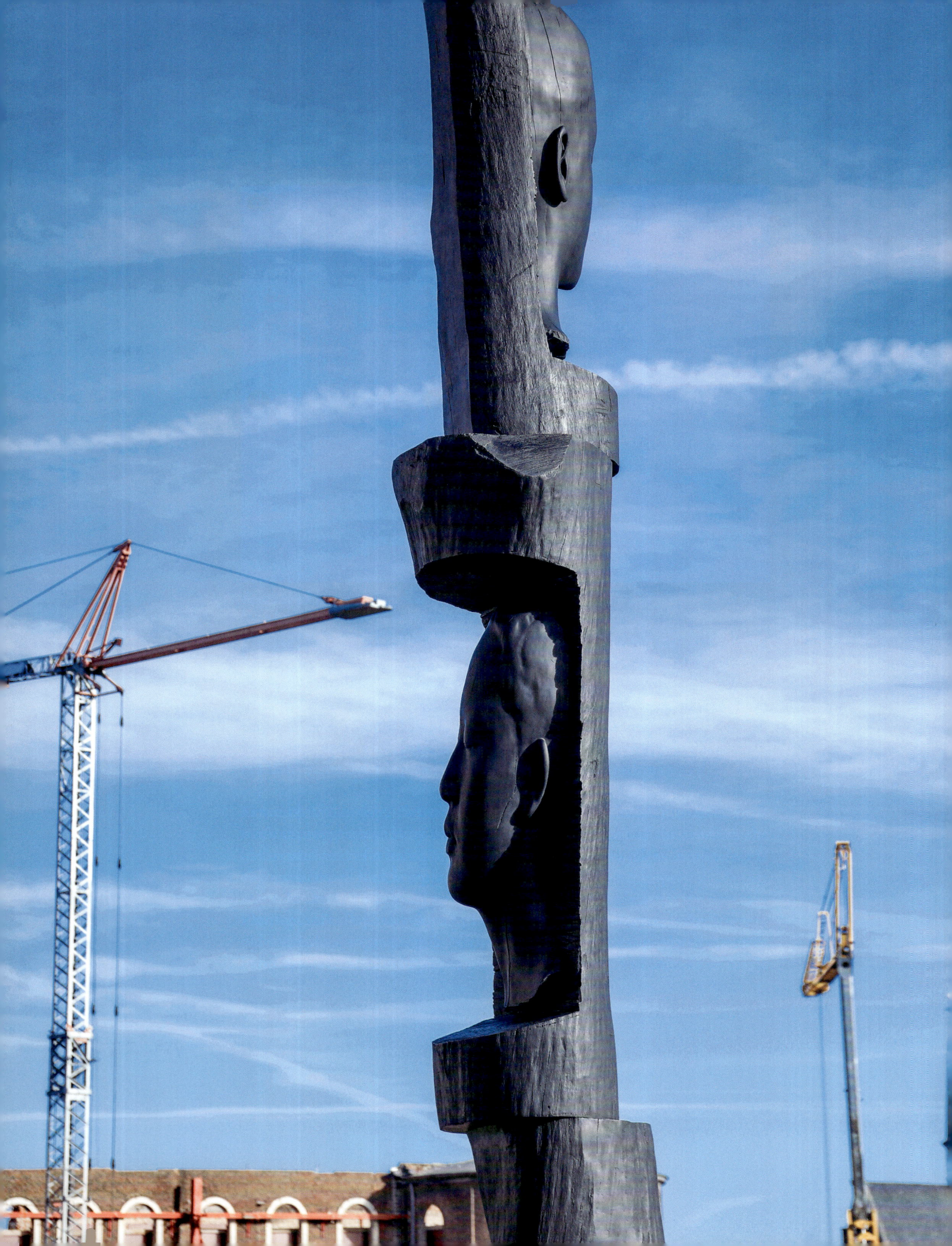

A Warm Welcome in Leuven

The paths of Leuven and its university have been running together for six centuries. Our history is intertwined: the city and the Alma Mater are often mentioned in the same breath. Leuven is a creative, innovative, and thriving city, curious, open-minded, and confidently focused on the world. Leuven owes much of the vibrant life to KU Leuven and its countless spin-off companies. And now our town has become also one of the proud places on earth to have Jaume Plensa's art in the public domain.

Humanists, scientists, and researchers have helped to put Leuven on the map. Erasmus, Vesalius, Mercator, and Lemaître are just a few of the world-renowned alumni. Leuven has been reconciling art, culture, and technology for centuries. It is a small town with big ambitions and a cosmopolitan character, indeed. A future laboratory for Europe, too.

The close ties between city and university are also noticeable in the shape of the city. Beautiful colleges, impressive libraries, a lively atmosphere thanks to the thousands of students. Tourist highlights such as Arenberg Castle or the Great Beguinage are part of both KU Leuven's and Leuven's heritage.

In the past, the university has enriched our city with several beautiful works of art. This is now happening again with *The Four Elements*, a monumental work consisting of two statues by Jaume Plensa. This Catalan artist is world-renowned for his sculptures in public spaces. Iconic places have thus become places of contemplation due to his intimate and thought-provoking heads and faces. With *The Four Elements*, in other words, Leuven now joins the ranks of New York, Madrid, Liverpool, and Tokyo, among others.

Plensa evokes the four elements – *Water, Earth, Air* and *Fire*– through powerfully elaborate heads in two specifically chosen locations: on the one hand, the Hertogen site – where Vesalius worked in the fifteenth century – and the University Library on Ladeuze Square, on the other. Plensa places the *Fire* element in the latter place for a clear reason: the University Library went up in flames during both world wars. The Great Fire of Leuven (1914) is one of the darkest pages in our history, and the destruction of the University Library led to worldwide outrage.

Art and culture for all is one of Leuven's aspirations. Art and culture are the driving forces for citizens to make plans together, to participate in the public sphere. That is why museums and cultural centers in Leuven are opening their doors, and the future Performing Arts Hall aims to be a living parlor for every inhabitant of Leuven. City festivals – another collaboration with the university – involve generations both new and old, reaching out to local associations and communities. Together we are (re)shaping the city.

Artistic creations in public spaces are an excellent way to make culture accessible to everyone. They literally bring art to the streets, to the people. Murals and sculptures make people wonder, raise questions, and even sometimes challenge people. They invite us to think and to dream and to come closer to one another. Self-knowledge through artistic experiences is an ideal basis for reflecting on our relationship with the other – who may be nearby or far away – and, hence, with society at large. Art that re- and interconnects us offers ideal opportunities for inclusive citizenship and solidarity in society. Thus, *The Four Elements* provides a new and fascinating chapter in the story of Leuven.

Mohamed Ridouani
Mayor of Leuven

Bert Cornillie
Alderman for Culture and Events

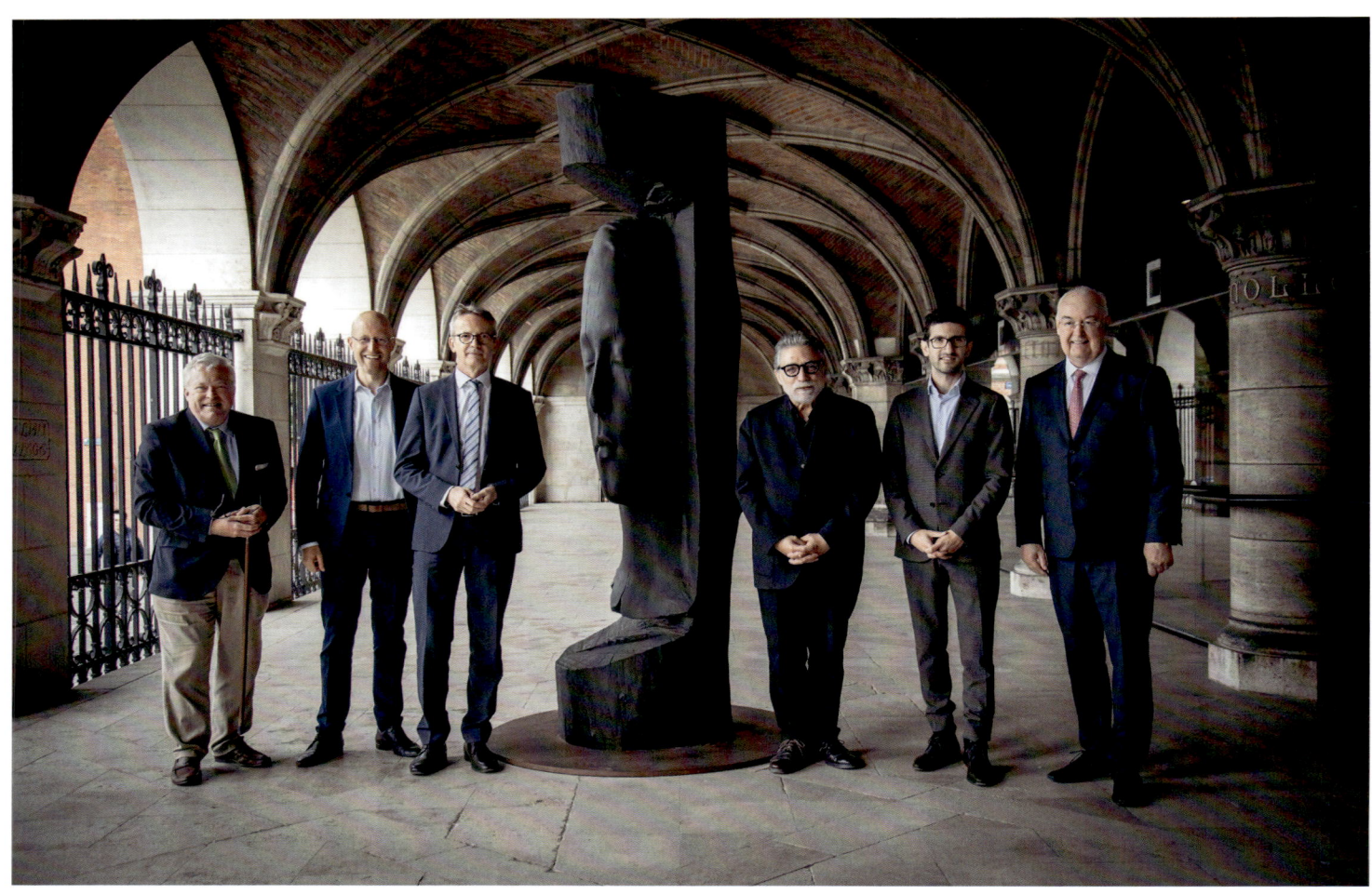

From left to right: Geert Bouckaert, Bert Cornillie, Luc Sels, Jaume Plensa, Mohamed Ridouani, Urbain Vandeurzen © Rob Stevens

The Four Elements

In her work *A Longing for Inconsolability* (1994), our late colleague Patricia de Martelaere presents twelve essays on themes such as life and death, art, writing, speaking and reading, the color of sounds, fiction in literature, and the uses of philosophy. In a Montaigne-like manner she takes us on a philosophical, reflexive tour of melancholy, art, words, language, and literature. It is a tour confronting us with our humanity, our uncertainties, our fears, our hopes, our longing for emptiness and fulfillment, our search for understanding and insight. Confronted with the cunning of uncertainty, as coined by Helga Novotny in 2015, it is a call for ever more profound knowledge, for a quest to push the knowledge frontier, to increase the body of knowledge on which we build our future. This is what universities are for. Places where humanity is at liberty to deconstruct and to construct knowledge. Places where the body of knowledge is safeguarded, registered, archived, revisited, rethought, recombined, created and recreated. Places that are simultaneously intensely local and fiercely global.

As the boundaries of the body of knowledge are in continuous flux, the ancient dimensions of earth, air, water, and fire come to mind. Claudius Ptolemaeus, who initiated them, considered them to be related to states of mood rather than being physical or chemical building blocks. In the meantime, and as a consequence of our thirst for knowledge, those ancient insights have been complemented, supplemented, and superseded. While Ptolemaeus's *Almagest* would for over one thousand years support both the Arab and Western view on the geocentric universe, it took Copernicus, Galileo, and Kepler significant intellectual courage and scientific effort to question and revolutionize this worldview. Even later, Thomas Kuhn was among the first to document such paradigmatic shifts in his authoritative work *The Structure of Scientific Revolutions* (University of Chicago Press, 1962), famously quoting Max Planck: "Old theories die because their proponents die."

Those knowledge dynamics explain the choice for Jaume Plensa's sculptures across the KU Leuven city campus. For 600 years, the university has contributed to the advancement of knowledge. KU Leuven has pioneered scientific breakthroughs in areas as diverse as the humanities, the social sciences, various fields of science and technology, and biomedicine, resulting in impactful new views on societal dynamics, technology developments, medical treatments, and novel drugs. Since the fifteenth century, KU Leuven has been home to scholars from the four corners of the globe to create new knowledge, revisit existing theories, and construct new ones. Jaume Plensa's *Body of Knowledge*, highlighting the four elements, is a fitting tribute to this relentless quest for knowledge and scientific insight. This relevancy explains why the board of Stichting Amici Almae Matris enthusiastically decided to support this initiative of KU Leuven's *Opening the future* campaign board. Through its generous donors, the campaign stimulates scientific breakthroughs in the neurosciences and oncology. Our scientists work at the forefront of the bodies of knowledge with which they engage. Jaume Plensa's sculptures are an homage to their efforts, the curiosity, and the generosity that enable them.

Plensa's sculptures also highlight the crossroads at which a comprehensive university operates. KU Leuven has always been a place where the two cultures as described by Charles Snow in 1956 ("The Two Cultures," in the *New Statesman*) co-exist, blend, and cross-fertilize: humanities and sciences, rather than humanities versus sciences. This co-existence and blending enable and sustain a rich academic culture – sometimes antagonistic, but ultimately always reinforcing and strengthening. Their different approaches to intellectual inquiry and method reinforce one another, rather than counteract or act in isolation. The four elements represented by the sculptures point to those constructive and productive interactions. Charles Snow's two cultures are joint protagonists, rather than antagonists. The current challenges and wicked problems facing humanity – to which the world of academic science further intends to contribute and, while doing so, make a difference – signal that our body of knowledge is incomplete and underdeveloped. The sculptures by Jaume Plensa build on the rich tradition of our Alma Mater. Scientific inquiry will enlighten humanity. Let *The Four Elements* be stimuli to this never ending quest, turning inconsolability into consolation, striving for a better world.

Filip Abraham
Chair, on behalf of the board of Stichting Amici Almae Matris

Koenraad Debackere
President, KU Leuven Association

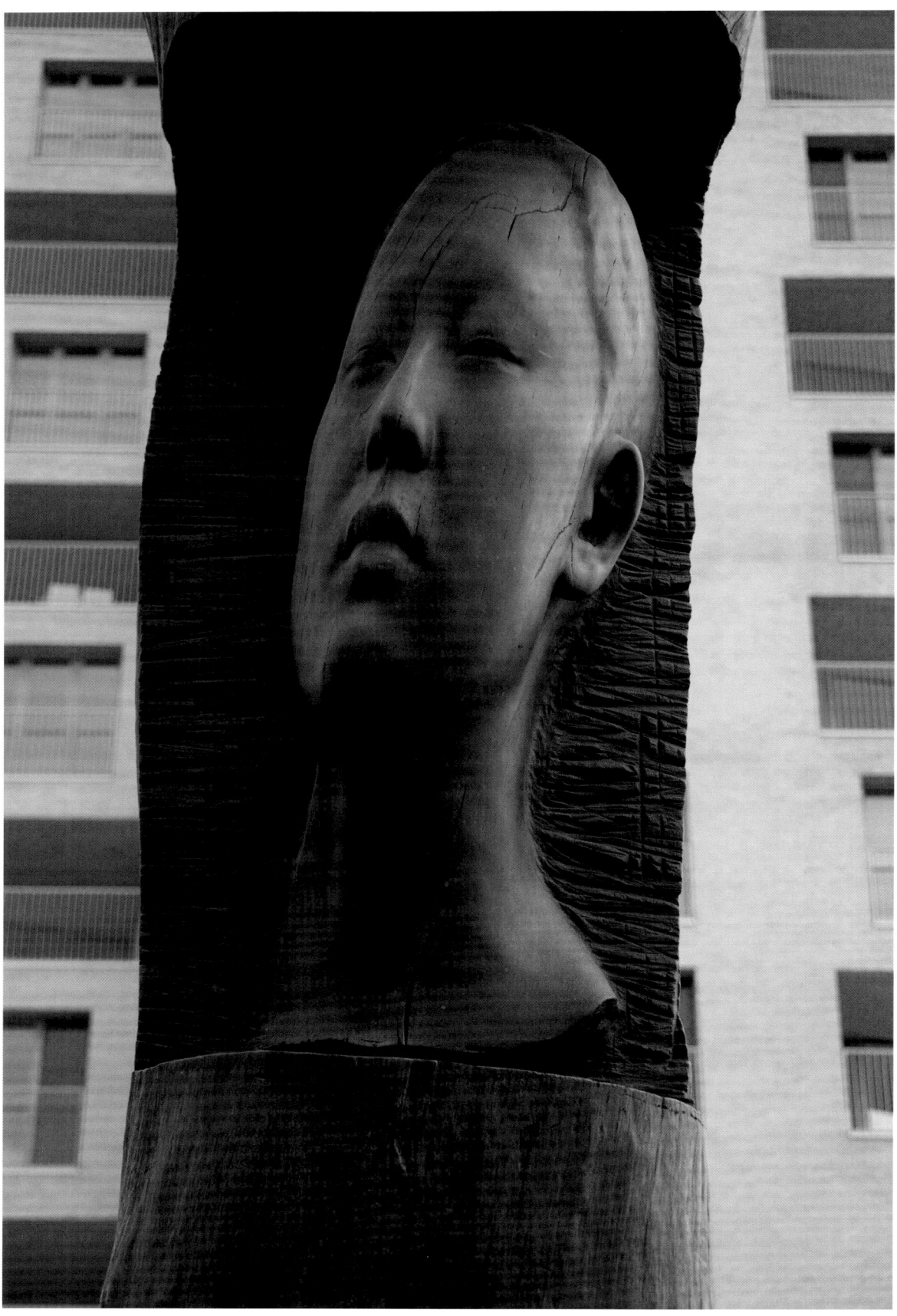

Stéphane Symons in Conversation with Jaume Plensa

The conversation took place at the University Library, KU Leuven, February 1, 2024

Stéphane Symons: Mr. Plensa, let me first congratulate you with this new work, *The Four Elements*, for which we are truly grateful. Rather than straightforwardly asking you for an 'explanation' of this new piece, I would like to present you with a quotation from a poem by T.S. Eliot. I know you cherish his work.

> At the still point of the turning world. Neither flesh nor fleshless;
> Neither from nor towards; at the still point, there the dance is,
> But neither arrest nor movement. And do not call it fixity,
> Where past and future are gathered. Neither movement from
> nor towards,
> Neither ascend nor decline. Except for the point, the still point,
> There will be no dance, and there is only the dance.
> I can only say, there we have been: but I cannot say where.
> And I cannot say, how long, for that is to place it in time.
> (*Burnt Norton*, *Four Quartets*)

Could this search for a "still point of the turning world" be related to your own artistic project? Are your works, including *The Four Elements*, spaces of stillness in the midst of a busy environment?

Jaume Plensa: Well, anything coming from T. S. Eliot is wonderful. It doesn't matter which poem. It's true that I often refer to *The Waste Land*, especially to its marvelous first lines: "April is the cruellest month, breeding / Lilacs out of the dead land."

The connection between my artworks and their surroundings is indeed very important. Their connection should be as organic as possible. To me, art should be closely intertwined with the public space in which it is installed. This does not mean that I create public art: art is always public. I'm creating art in public spaces, which is something different.

The connection between KU Leuven and the city of Leuven is organic in the same way. I was touched by the fact that, in Leuven, you don't know where the university starts and the city ends. It is very clear that there is a shared commitment between the university and the city. Every time I met your rector, Luc Sels, his involvement with the city was obvious, and, vice versa, your mayor Mohamed Ridouani follows closely what the university is doing. This permanent conversation between the university and the city is amazing and exceptional.

Symons: In previous interviews, you have referred to the importance of silence, which opens up a different meaning of the word "still." One element from *The Four Elements*, the element *Fire*, was installed at the entrance of the University Library, obviously a "still" and quiet place.

Plensa: *The Four Elements* are indeed installed at two different locations: in St. Raphaël's Square and at the entrance of the University Library. With the installation at the library, I did not just want to draw attention to the beauty or strength of the piece, but also to the emptiness behind it. The corridor in which it was installed is totally empty, and that was very important. But my work is above all a memory of many things. Firstly, it commemorates the history of the library, which was burned several times for senseless reasons. Even the color of the piece is somewhat remindful of the black color of burnt things. But the concentration and stillness that is key to the users of the library is very relevant as well. The female figure in my piece has closed eyes. This is normal in my work because I want to emphasize the richness that we keep inside. I want to evoke the beauty we are hiding inside ourselves, which we do not communicate to others. And then there is the loneliness of the figure in the empty hall. The building is so majestic, and the sculpture is alone in this amazing area. The work was meant as a gesture to welcome the users of the library, and I hope it can work like a mirror in which one can reflect oneself. That has always been important in my work.

Symons: I find this reference to the importance of emptiness very intriguing. Artists create new objects and add novel things to an already crowded world. Every artwork inevitably *takes up* space. But your work is very modest. Because emptiness plays such an important role, your work almost seems to take a step back. It does not force itself onto the viewer. It does not so much take up space as *create* space – a space to think, to feel, to interact with one another.

Plensa: I have always defended a very classical attitude. My work is primarily an excuse to study space in a different way, to look at the urban context or at nature. I think a sculptor has a tremendous capacity to expand energy. For this, the actual object is less important than what it produces in its environment. In the library, I aimed to encourage dialogue rather than to provoke shock. Nowadays, so much work revolves around shock or provocation.

My work tries to be silent and seeks to invite people to keep silent as well. In such a dialogue, which does not need any words, we exchange energy. I'm creating silence in a very noisy time. This has always been one of my obsessions. Not the silence of 'shutting up' but a poetic concept of silence that allows us to feel a certain vibration, to reconnect with our thoughts. We are receiving so many messages all the time that we perhaps end up no longer speaking our own thoughts. We repeat, as an echo, the things that come to us from without. This worries me because we hardly take the time to think about our reactions to these messages.

I know that it sounds like a contradiction when I refer to the need to create silence in the public domain. Or when I say that I am setting up an intimate relationship with the audience. But I think it's possible and it's working. I'm trying not to talk to the community, but to each and every individual in front of my work. Of course these individuals make up a community together, but I'm interested in every-one of those people, individually. Art is a message to be read personally. You can never fully share your feelings. And this is very important, even in the public space. I have often had the positive experience that people react in a very special way and bring about an intimate moment that lasts a few seconds. This is enough to enable them to think about themselves and about their emotions.

Symons: In previous interviews you have used the metaphor of different islands that are connected by a bridge. Can art be a bridge that brings together individuals?

Plensa: Yes. For me, individuals are like islands that can be connected. Celebrating life means celebrating diversity. And all human beings are unique. When one human being disappears, a big library is gone. An enormous amount of information. Hundreds of computers, memories, things that can never be brought back. This is why I will never understand people who think war could be a solution for anything. Any decision that means that somebody could die is wrong. We ought to celebrate life, diversity. How beautiful it is to be different, but together. This conviction is rooted in yet another contradiction, that is, in the awareness that we are not perfect. This awareness of imperfection is an incredible engine for moving forward into the future. If we were perfect, we would be dead. The beauty of humanity lies in our constant pursuit of trying something new.

Symons: You once mentioned that every sculpture asks its own question. Which question is asked by *The Four Elements*?

Plensa: That is difficult for me to know. When the work was inaugurated, I addressed the audience and told them that, from that moment onwards, the work would be theirs. And I asked them to take good care of it. This does not just entail physically respecting the piece. It entails starting to ask questions. But I cannot know which questions these will be.

What is more, my works are always fragments of something more complex. They are like parts of a body: a foot, a hand, an eye, a tongue, an ear. These body parts are all very different. How can you imagine that one's feet and eyes are part of the same body? That they work together? This metaphor of the body is often used to describe societies, and I like that idea a lot. I do not want to engage in a kind of journalism, showing reality as it is. I do not just want to describe what has happened. That would be too easy. I want to offer ideas of hope. I want to send out messages of hope, perhaps very risky ones, because we are not perfect. In the context of KU Leuven, I wanted to talk about the four elements because these are the origin of everything: fire, water, air, earth. That is the real beginning. Everything is built up from there.

Symons: Your interest in the smallest building blocks of creation is striking in the context of a discussion of sculpture, an art form that is usually associated with monumentality and size. Your sculptures do not aim for spectacle. They build up effect by bringing together different, smaller pieces. You created works that consist of two pieces (e.g., *Night and Day*, *Mirror*) and works that consist of three pieces (e.g., *Three Graces*). Was *The Four Elements*, consisting of four 'building blocks,' a logical, next step?

Plensa: For some reason, the number four is important to me. As you know, I love poetry. I have been using a lot of poetic texts. Four poets are like the four legs of my table on which I build: Shakespeare, Blake, Dante, and Baudelaire. This list was later expanded with other poets: William Carlos Williams, T.S. Eliot, many others. But it did start with four. *The Four Elements* that I created here in Leuven can also be regarded as four legs to build on. It prepares a next step and remains open.

As you mentioned, I like the idea of combining smaller things to create a more complex organism. In the end, this is also how our bodies operate, with various body parts that work together. And this is how language works. Texts are made up of words, and words are made up of single letters. This structural similarity between the human body and language is important in my work. For me, the voice is the music of the human body.

We always go from the smaller to the greater. We are constantly surrounded by small things that are brought together to make something big. That is my preferred image of the cosmos.

Symons: It is also the structure of a library. The University Library is a monumental building, but what would it be without the thousands of books? Without all those small components that somehow work together?

Plensa: Indeed. You could call it a biological outlook on life. Small cells bring about high degrees of complexity.

Symons: You just mentioned the structural resemblance of the human body and language. Your work is indeed known for combining the shape of the human body with letters and words. In works like *Soul* or *Body of Knowledge*, human bodies are made entirely of language. *The Four Elements* does not include letters or words. But three of its elements (*Water, Earth, Air*) were

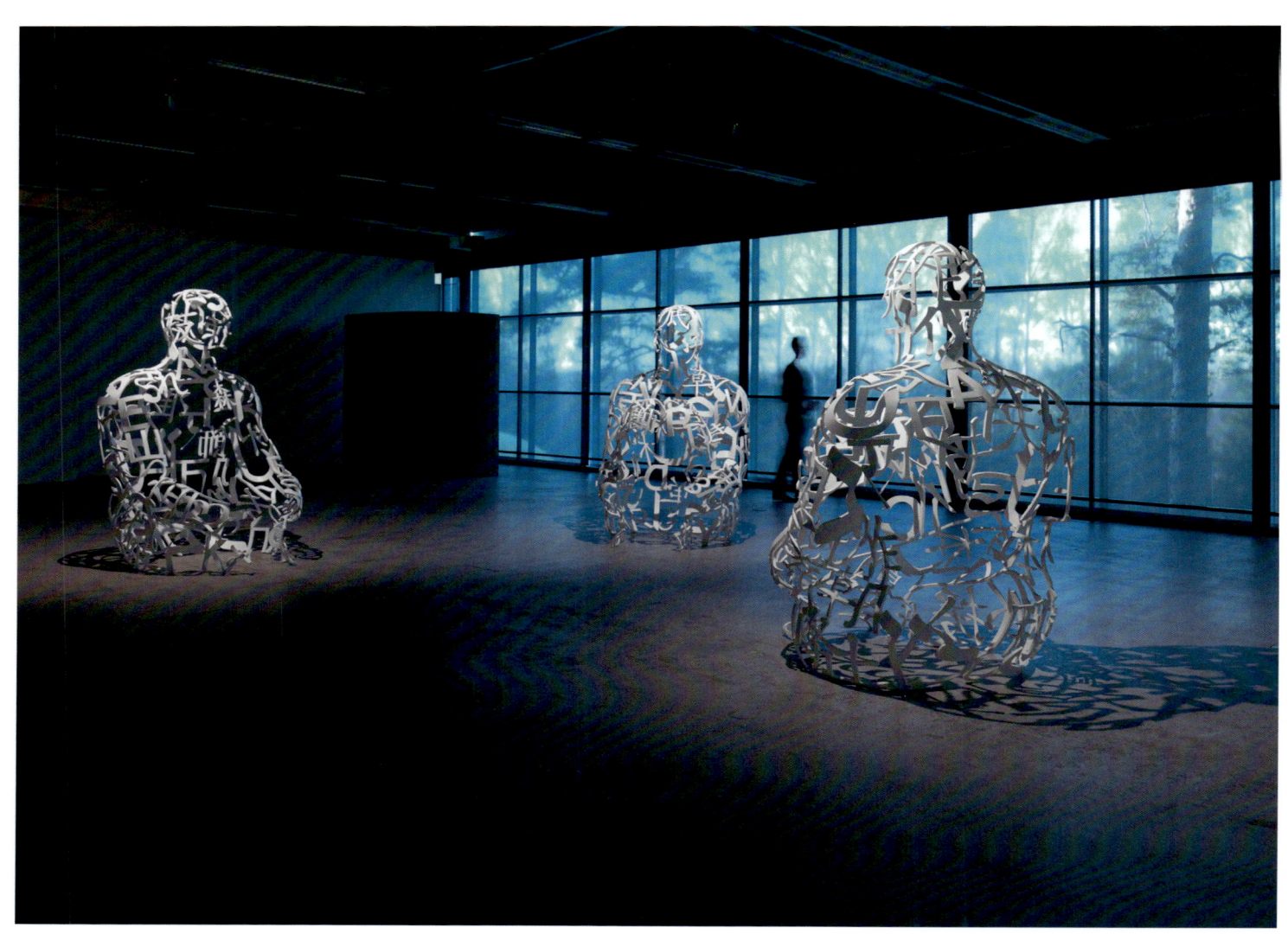

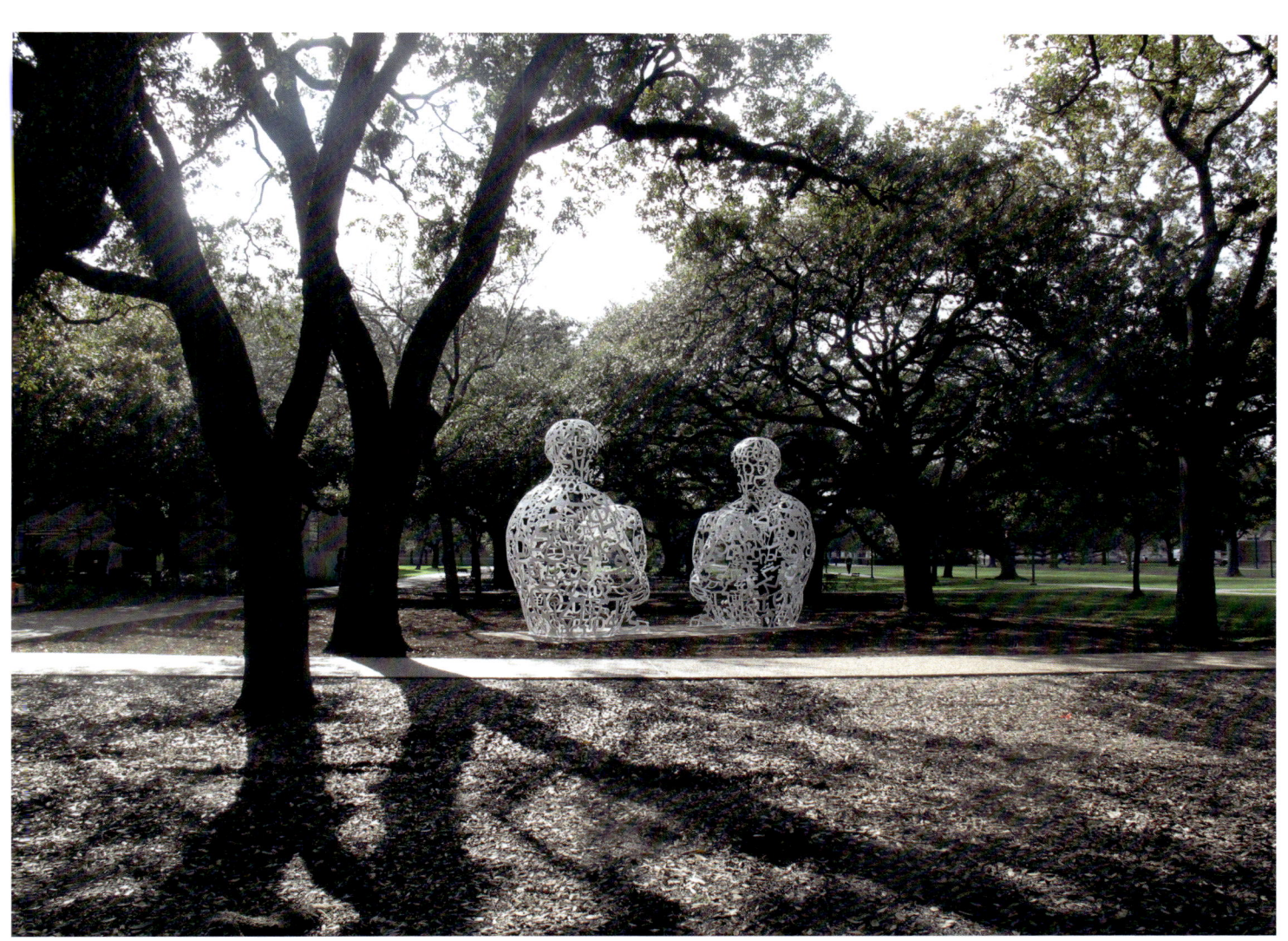

installed in the vicinity of the new Vesalius Center, focused on the many facets of the human body, and one element (*Fire*) was installed at the entrance of the library. Can one argue that the connection between body and text is thus maintained here as well?

Plensa: *Body of Knowledge* was created in 2010 for the Goethe University in Frankfurt. It is a very big piece made up of letters. These are my obsessions [*laughs*]. But in Leuven, I wanted to change direction a little bit and explore something even more elemental and basic. What was before the text? This brought me to the four elements. With the 600th anniversary of KU Leuven in mind, I wanted to invite a conversation about the beginning of everything. In the very beginning, there were the four elements. Perhaps the university was expecting a work with text, but I decided to jump and do something different. And I'm very happy with what I did. It's closer to my feelings today.

Symons: By referring to an elemental world that predates language, your work also opens the discussion about the fragility of the body of knowledge. All those words that build up knowledge and complexity – they can also be destroyed.

Plensa: Yes, this is highly relevant in a library that was burned down twice. An image that I like a lot is that, after everything was burned, nothing disappeared completely. The power of memory enables human beings to recover from the most tragic events. I was very impressed when reading about the tragic moments in the history of the KU Leuven. The resilience and ability to recover, again and again, is very powerful. For me, that really was an incredible metaphor.

Symons: What were the motivations behind your decision to divide the work in two pieces? Why did you want to install part of the work in the library and part of it in St. Raphaël's Square? Moreover, those four elements, or four faces, all look in opposite directions.

Plensa: In St. Raphaël's Square, I wanted to install a totem, linked to very old traditions originating in Native American cultures in North America. I am very fascinated with ritual totems and the images of animals or magic

IMAGINATION IS MORE IMPORTANT THAN KNOWLEDGE

elements. But I've always considered human beings to be the most magical and strongest of all gods. That is the main reason why I've been using heads of female figures. Always in a dream-like state, turned inward. These heads are indeed looking in different directions, but they are not facing anything in particular. They are concentrated on the inside. That is a contradiction. It is very important to me that these heads resonate a sovereignty, a certain independency vis-à-vis their immediate surroundings.

In the totem, I also wanted to create an effect of displacement. Because the different heads are stacked as a totem, this makes for a fragile view. An instructor-engineer might get worried. [*laughs*] It is not a perfectly vertical column. But that effect is part of my take on human fragility and of the awareness that even the most monumental things can fall down.

We were also in luck that there is water nearby. I have often installed work near water, even in rivers, in the sea, in the ocean. At St. Raphaël's Square, there might not be an ocean, but there is a wonderful river that is visible again. The bronze of the totem is forever fixed in that size, in that weight, in that context. But the water will never be the same. One sometimes hears the saying that water is the only thing one cannot see twice because it's always moving. But my piece is not complete either. The fourth element is in the library. It refers to books and to the power of memory. And this fourth installment is required to complete the work. I like that a lot.

Symons: Your suggestion that all monumental things retain a certain fragility can also be inverted: what seems fragile and precarious can nonetheless embody a certain strength. That certainly seems to be case with the female faces in *The Four Elements*. The work also brought to mind the series of sculptures in Karnak, which are important to you.

Plensa: Yes, what I like so much in Karnak is the beauty of repetition. The series becomes like a rhythm, like a harmony. *The Four Elements* also thrives on repetition. One element is repeated four times. Three elements are mounted on top of each other; the fourth one is installed at a different location. But the faces are different. These are four different women from different places in the world. When I use text, I use different alphabets from different places. Similarly, the four women in *The Four Elements* originate from different places.

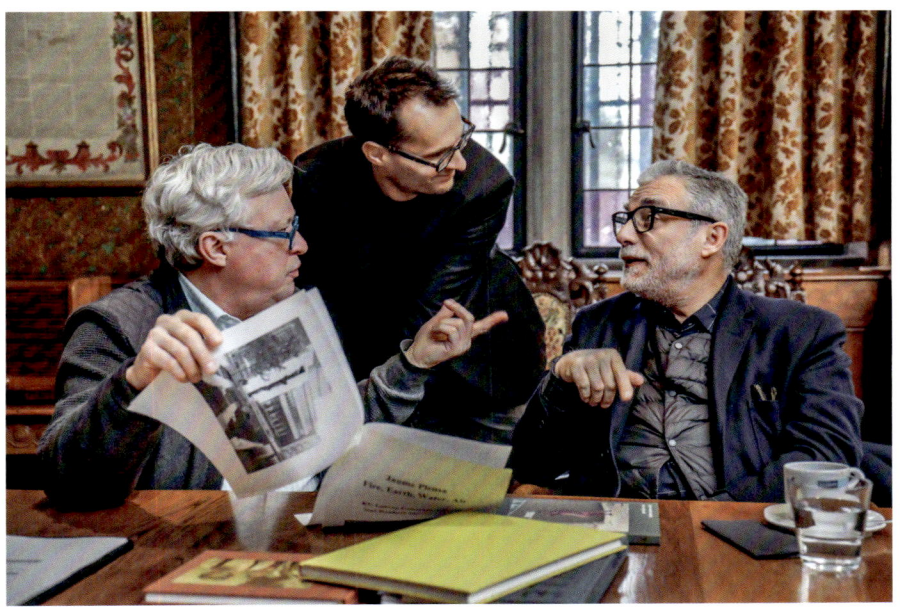

Geert Bouckaert (left), Stéphane Symons (middle) and Jaume Plensa (right) in conversation.
© Rob Stevens.

But I will not say too much about the piece. It has opened its own path. What I would really like is that, one day, people will say to one another: "Shall we meet by the river? Shall we meet where there are the three faces?" Maybe, at some point, the inhabitants of Leuven will give the work a new name. The work will only be really successful when it will be completely integrated in the everyday life of the inhabitants of the city. My hope is that it can create a point of repair. That it works like a beacon. Pieces that are installed at the precise crossing of two streets and a bridge can clearly be seen from four different points. Especially at night. It is very pretty when illuminated.

Symons: The interaction between science and art is an important part of KU Leuven's intellectual agenda. What are your views on the relationship between both?

Plensa: When I was very young, I read a text by the French mathematician René Thom, which I found incredibly fascinating. And the work of Einstein helped me a lot in many special moments of my life. He was so clever and yet so easy to understand. A very powerful man. I have much admiration for scientists because they are able to progress step by step. I find that very difficult, I'm too chaotic. [*laughs*]

It is true that a dialogue between science and art works tremendously well. Both are not afraid to talk about what is invisible. They both have a poetic dimension, one coming from an interest in materiality, the other from an interest in spirituality. But there is no such thing as spirit without materiality. There is no soul without a body. Science can be likened to a body and art to a soul, and together they create something entirely different.

As I mentioned earlier, bodies are very important to me. The human body in particular. I have a lot of friends who are medical doctors. We often discuss shared interests. And when I'm in a hospital, it is clear that the presence of nature – say, a garden and trees – has a beneficial effect on the recovery process of the patients. The presence of art can have a similar impact. I'm trying to increase the awareness of beauty in this strange time and world, and science has the capacity to create better living conditions. Let us collaborate more.

Symons: Talking about successful collaborations between scientists and artists, it is important to mention the crucial role of [the campaign] *Opening the future*. *The Four Elements* pays tribute to its pioneering work and the cutting-edge brain research that it supports. In past interviews, you have often talked about the specific role of the human brain. In your view it is not just the seat of rationality but also the "wildest part of the body." What did you mean with this, and how is this idea relevant to your work?

Plensa: You are right, this project is an homage to brain research and the fight against brain diseases like Alzheimer's. I want to help raise awareness.

I have indeed often mentioned that the brain is the wildest part of our bodies. If two ideas want to come together in your brain, they will meet. Even if you don't like it [*laughs*]. When we're in good health, this is a very poetic idea. But, sadly, it is true that so many people suffer from brain diseases like Alzheimer's. Also in my immediate surroundings. I don't know if this has always been the case, but today it seems very striking. Sometimes our bodies are in good health, but our brains aren't.

I believe that artistic creation is capable of impacting the brain by creating common memories. I continue to create elements that we can share.

These elements do not necessarily have a purely intellectual or rational aspect. Rather, I'm bringing about emotions and want to enable as many people as possible to relate with my work. My work is primarily directed to people with a big heart. Ordinary people who have a wish to participate in something new, something that can be loved together. I do think this contributes to a better society. The wildness of the public domain, in contrast to museums and galleries, is important here. There is always the chance that something unknown can happen. My pieces will have to survive by themselves. There is no context that protects them. People will not have looked for this work. It will just be there, unexpected. There are plenty of things that I'm trying to say in my work. But, above all, it is directed to human beings who want to create a shared memory, with me and with the rest of society.

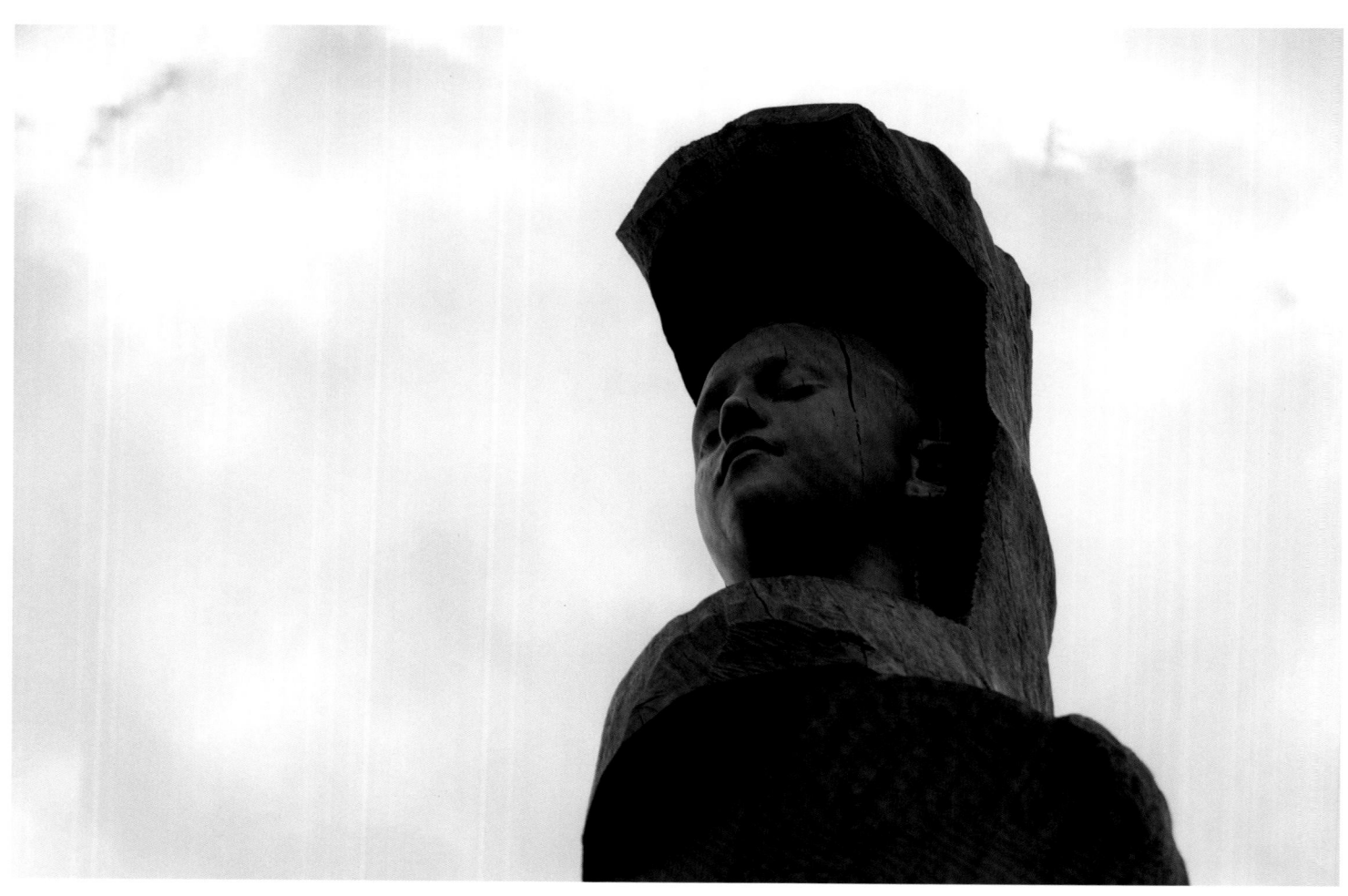

Eyes Wide Shut
One Theme, with a Dozen
Associations around
The Four Elements

Johan Wagemans

A dozen associations

With its rich and dense network of connections to the university and the public space in which it is situated, Plensa's sculpture *The Four Elements* triggers a great deal of associations in my thinking about it. I mention a dozen but discuss only six, all centered around one main theme.

When I first saw pictures of Plensa's sculpture, three characteristics stood out to me. First, the central figure, repeated in all four of the sculpture's main components is a *female bust*. Second, the piece on St. Raphaël's Square resembles a *totem* – a stacked series of three almost identical, but subtly distinct, female busts. Third is the aspect of *traces*. Because we are told to consider the two main pieces together as one integrated sculpture consisting of four elements, as emphasized by its title, there are obvious traces between the single bust in the gallery of the University Library and the three stacked busts on St. Raphaël's Square. In addition, there are traces between the statues and their local context: the *Sedes Sapientiae*; the University Library, along with its associated collective knowledge; and the new Vesalius Museum, with its links to medicine, health, and the University

Hospital. Furthermore, the piece in the gallery of the University Library will also relate – whether it wants this or not – with Jan Fabre's *Totem*, especially through its associated totem-like sister piece. Finally, because each of the female heads is oriented in different directions, they also suggest traces or paths throughout the city.

The next set of three associations, which I mention only briefly here, are central to my work as an experimental psychologist specialized in visual perception. The *eyes* are the organs through which we receive visual stimulation from the environment, and they are also salient visual elements in the four female heads (to be discussed in more detail below). The way the eyes operate is strongly linked to the *brain*, both by how it receives and processes the sensations registered by the eyes and by how it steers the muscles to move the eyes, which is needed to continuously feed itself with new sensations. In fact, the cones and rods, the receptors in the two retinae that capture the light, are generally considered by neuroscientists to function as an extension of the brain. For a psychologist, vision is not just the human window onto the world – the way in which the organism gains access to its environment in order to be able to behave adaptively – but also the scientist's window onto our *mind*. Perception constitutes one of the most obvious forms of the mind-body problem: what enters as light and is transmitted through chemical and electrical receptor and neural activity somehow turns into a subjective perception with a particular shape, color, distance, and meaning. Centuries of neuroanatomy and neurophysiology, as well as decades of brain scanning, multi-unit, single-cell and subcellular recording have not been able to unravel where, when, and how the physical signals are turned into our awareness of things in the world that could have caused them. At best, we have only been able to establish some quantitative psycho-physiological relationships between characteristics of the stimuli and our responses to them. The qualities of our subjective experience remain notoriously difficult to grasp by our standard ways of doing science.

Leaving aside these two sets of three general associations with the artwork and three general associations with the perception of it, I will now turn to a more substantial discussion of two other sets of three more specific associations, centered around one central theme: the most obvious fact that the eyes of all female heads in *The Four Elements* are closed and all the possible implications this composition might have for our perception of the sculpture.

The 1,000 words that open and closed eyes can speak

In our everyday life, eyes are important vehicles of social communication because they are "the window into the soul." Our own eyes convey our reactions and emotions – and sometimes our thoughts and intentions – whether we want it or not. Because of this response, we also use what we see in someone else's eyes as crucial information about their feelings and states of mind. By paying attention to a person's gaze – the direction in which their eyes look – we can infer what they are looking at and therefore paying attention to. Through a process of "joint attention," even young children can share their attention with their caregivers' attention;[1] learn to pick up important characteristics of what matters in their environment; and even determine what words refer to when they are used to categorize things, scenes, and events in the world.[2] A deficit in joint attention has often been suggested as an early marker of autism,[3] because it would hamper the development of a "theory of mind" – an implicit understanding of what another person feels, thinks, or wants.[4]

No surprise, then, that photographs of people often have very telling eyes and that artists have long been depicting eyes in portraits to convey information about a person, their emotions, intentions, and even personality. Because of its important role in Plensa's artwork, I will use several examples about the use of eyes as vehicles of communication in photography, paintings, and sculptures – the third set of three associations. The pictures will mainly speak for themselves.

Photography
We read a great deal of feelings, thoughts, and states of mind into depicted (pairs of) eyes. I refer to three photographs that illustrate a strong gaze right into the lens and yet, each of them seems to convey a different message. In "Boy Holding Puppy" by André Kertesz, a boy shows his puppy dog, seemingly ambivalent, simultaneously self-assured, yet expressing a kind of wait-and-see attitude (see: https://bit.ly/4b5npHI). "Laila" by Abdel Gani Mohammad Radi shows a girl with piercing green eyes gazes serene but determined (see: https://bit.ly/45plVXK), and in Ulla Deventer's portrait of a sex worker in Ghana, a woman looks somewhat defiant to the beholder (see: https://bit.ly/3VrneRg).

Two other photographs illustrate two different type of gazes in which the person looks in a distinct way. "After Hours' by Corey Critser depicts a lady fully concentrated on her stitching (see: https://bit.ly/45l5RGB). "Scarred" by Natalie Arber shows a lady with a scarred neck stares straight ahead, probably into a mirror (see: https://bit.ly/3VrnmQK).

Even when they are not fully visible, we read a great deal of feelings, thoughts, and states of mind into depicted (pairs of) eyes. Photographs depicting pairs or groups of people add another layer of communication as is shown in a still depicting a scene with Humphrey Bogart and Ingrid Bergman from the movie Casablanca (see: https://bit.ly/4eAFGQv). Even though there's only one eye open, one closed (or looking downward), and one eyelash, the viewer immediately notices that the couple looks into each other's eyes, where the mouths add a tone of sadness. Is this a goodbye? Another example the third picture from the photo series Italian Gangsters by Peter Lindbergh (see: https://bit.ly/3xpLviD). It depicts four young ladies around a table full of food. All of them have their eyes down or their gaze averted away from the camera and one another, clearly demonstrating how strongly they are lost in their own thoughts. The four men in the back, shot at low-contrast, only raise our desire to know what is going on. Is this an innocent moment of reflection before the party starts, or some serious trouble looming on the horizon?

Closed or downward looking eyes do not remain silent; they also reveal something about the person's intention, avoiding eye contact for instance or mental condition such as feeling ashamed or being absorbed in reflective thought.

Paintings

For centuries, painters have skillfully painted eyes with all sorts of expressions and messages as well. The portraits in figure 1 show only a fraction of what is possible: (a) the young man with the red hat painted by Jan Mostaert just stares ahead, seemingly sunk into his own thinking; while (b) the man with the black hat, known as *The Laughing Cavalier* by Frans Hals, is clearly much more self-assured. His eyes are looking at us from a side view and subtly smile at us; whereas (c) the young woman painted by Marie Denise Villers stares directly at us and – because she is probably drawing or painting what she is looking at– she draws us viewers even more strongly into the painting. This technique of involving the viewer in the painting has become a real theme in art throughout history. The following examples of self-portraits demonstrate how strongly painters are aware of the role of eyes in portraits. In several famous cases, the painters explicitly avoid painting their own eyes: by not showing their eyes like for example Giorgio Morandi (see: https://bit.ly/3VF4Ndo), by hiding them behind dark glasses like Pierre Bonnard and Mark Rothko (see: https://bit.ly/3Vgvi7u and https://bit.ly/4bWNDxx), by deforming them like Léon Spilliaert (see: https://bit.ly/4en4ECr), or by showing them in a skull like James Ensor (see: https://bit.ly/3VF4Kye). One could interpret this maneuver as not willing to provide us a look into their souls or as a trick to escape from the impossibility of looking simultaneously into the mirror and at the canvas, where their brush tries to simulate what they see in the mirror. Self-portraits by painters are thus really about the (im)possibilities of seeing and not seeing, the duality of revealing and hiding.

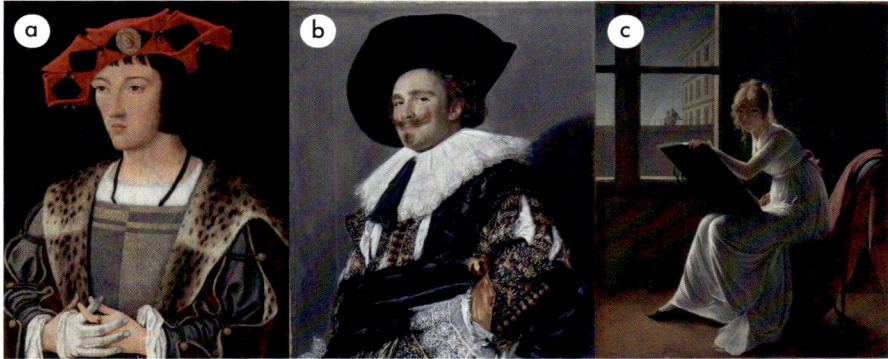

Figure 1. Paintings of Individual People with Telling Eyes.
(a) Jan Mostaert, *Portrait of a Man Putting on a Glove*, 1520.
(b) Frans Hals, *The Laughing Cavalier*, 1624.
(c) Marie Denise Villers, *Marie Josephine Charlotte du Val d'Ognes*, 1801.

The French Baroque painter Georges de la Tour has become quite famous, not only for his masterful play with light and dark (*chiaroscuro*) – revealing and hiding things by candle-lights put strategically in dark indoor scenes – but also for his playful suggestions of cheating and stealing in scenes with multiple people who clearly show what they are or are not looking at (see figures 2a and 2b). The theme of seeing versus not seeing

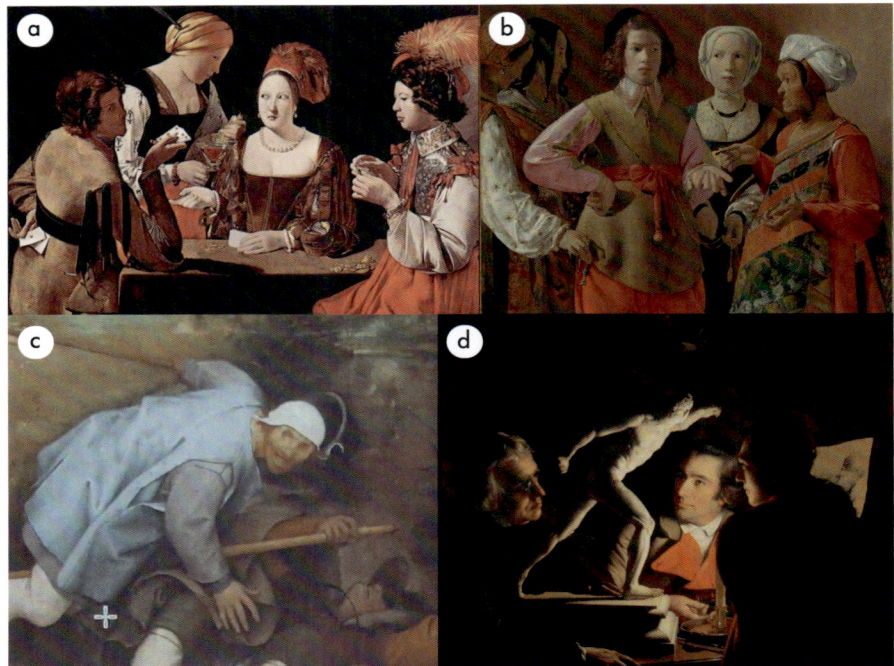

Figure 2. Images and Paintings of Pairs or Groups of People with Telling Eyes or Gazes.
(a) George de la Tour, *Cheating with an Ace at Cards*, 1630.
(b) George de la Tour, *The Fortune Teller*, ~1630s.
(c) Detail from Pieter Bruegel, *The Parable of the Blind*.
(d) Wright of Derby, *At the Light of a Candle, Three Men Study a Small Replica of the Borghese Gladiator*, 1765.

is even more explicit in the two other paintings illustrated in figure 2: (c) Bruegel's *Parable of the Blind* and (d) the scene of three men all looking at a male statue with its head turned away from the viewer, each with a different pair of eyes (both eyes shown, both eyes partially shown behind glasses, and only one eye shown).

A realistic depiction of eyes is notoriously difficult but not really necessary because we, as viewers, are so very used to seeing eyes and reading a great deal more into them than actually shown. Figure 3 (a) starts with a famous portrait by Vermeer of a lady with her head turned to us and staring at us, and then shows (b) a recent, hyper-realistic painting of a young man by a contemporary artist, Aline Verstraten (combining her background in psychology with her high degree of skillfulness in oil painting as crucial components for her PhD in the Arts at the University of Hasselt). In Vermeer's *Girl with the Red Hat*, the right eye of the lady is no more than an ellipse, half black, half pale brown, with a small white ellipse (depicting a highlight) positioned on the borderline between the two halves (Figure 3c). In Verstraten's *Knipogend* portrait, meanwhile, the right eye of the young man has all the anatomical details of a perfect human eye with all the necessary subtle shape and color features, as well as a bright highlight (figure 3d). In another famous painting (figure 3e), Vermeer hides the eye of the lady

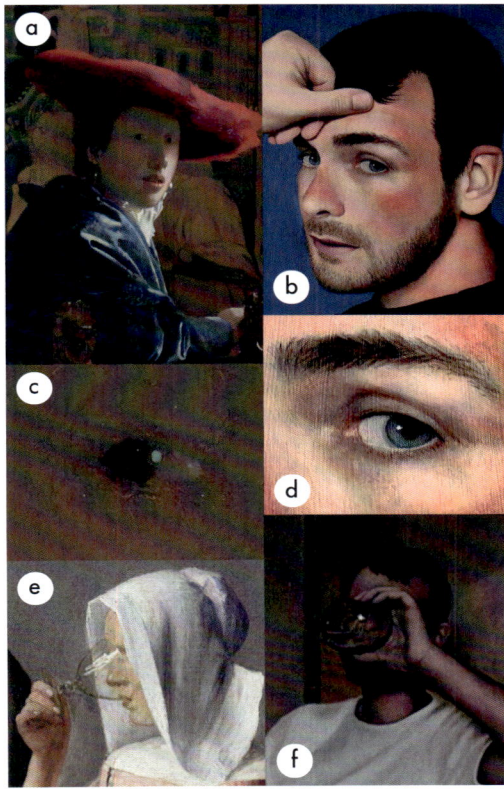

Figure 3. A Dialogue between Paintings With or Without Eyes by Vermeer and Verstraten.
(a) Johannes Vermeer, *Girl with the Red Hat*, c. 1669.
(b) Aline Verstraten, *Het Rood Trekt Nog Weg*, 2022. © Aline Verstraten.
(c) Detail from Johannes Vermeer, *Girl with the Red Hat*, c. 1669.
(d) Detail from Aline Verstraten, *Het Rood Trekt Nog Weg*, 2022. © Aline Verstraten.
(e) Detail from Johannes Vermeer, *The Glass of Wine*, 1661.
(f) Detail from Aline Verstraten, *Knipogen*, 2022. © Aline Verstraten.

with a white headscarf by the very salient highlight in the super-thin wine-glass, which is somehow mirrored by Verstraten's use of a focal point thrown by a strong beam of light, to suggest the location of the pupil of the man drinking water from a glass with a thick bottom (figure 3f). Verstraten's own description of the theme of revealing and hiding (or in this case, revealing by hiding) and how it fits into the central theme of her doctoral dissertation – the withdrawing image –constitute a valuable guide to a better understanding of the subtlety and complexity of her artwork and related paintings from the art-historical canon.[5] This theme has been exploited to its maximum by two pairs of her paintings: one self-portrait with the gaze directed at the viewer and one with a downward gaze (figure 4a and 4b), and one painting with a self-portrait viewed from the back on one side of the wooden panel, along with a portrait of her partner, also viewed from the back, on the other side of the same panel (figure 4c and 4d).

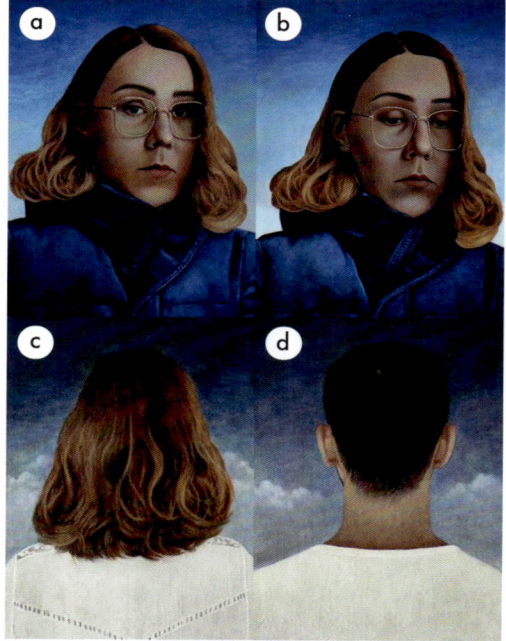

Figure 4. Two Pairs of Paintings With or Without Eyes by Aline Verstraten.
(a) and (b) Aline Verstraten, *Self-portrait*, 2023. © Aline Verstraten.
(c) and (d) Aline Verstraten, *Hier en Daar*, 2023. © Aline Verstraten.

Sculptures

Let us, finally, come to a brief discussion of open and closed eyes in sculpture. Because sculptures are volumetric and the human eye consists of an eyeball (a sphere) in a socket (a hole), with the pupil (an opening) surrounded by the iris (a colored ring) and an elliptic white part of the eyeball, the rendering of human eyes in sculptured portraits is quite difficult. When the eyes are sculpted in the head (figure 5a) – as in the bust of Helmholtz (one of the pioneers of vision science) by Hildebrand (a famous sculptor and friend, who also wrote about vision)[6] – they can look weird, because the convex part of the eyeball shows very little of its essence for us to understand the "looks" of the person and all the things we normally read into eyes when depicted in photographs or paintings. This is much less the case when the human figures all look down (figure 5b) or the eyes are painted-in by using color (figure 5c), as was often the case in earlier periods throughout art history. Some recent sculptures avoid this problem in subtler ways (figure 5d and 5e). Abstracted heads can work around this problem by merely leaving open spaces where eyes could fit (figure 5f).

Jaume Plensa's four female heads show various ways of keeping the eyes closed, all of which we probably interpret differently because of the subtle differences in the mouths below them. I would be interested in learning more about the artist's intentions with these variations and in empirically investigating how naïve viewers look at these heads, eyes, and mouths (through recording eye movements); how they interpret their expressions; and whether their interpretations align with the artist's intentions (through questionnaires and ratings). Humans are notorious experts in reading emotions from faces,[7] and they do not hesitate to attribute social positions and personality traits to the individuals whose faces they see.[8] Whether we are equally willing and able to do so for faces in paintings and sculptures, and what role is played by the eyes in them, has been much less well-studied, however. The discussion above clarifies that eyes (open or closed) and gazes (direct or averted, looking at the viewer or away from them) all communicate a range of messages. Artists will also know about these communicative powers and the effects they could have on their viewers. Empirical research aimed at understanding this dialogue would be quite interesting. I hope to contribute to answering some of these open questions, with regards to Plensa's *The Four Elements*, soon after its official installation and opening to the public.

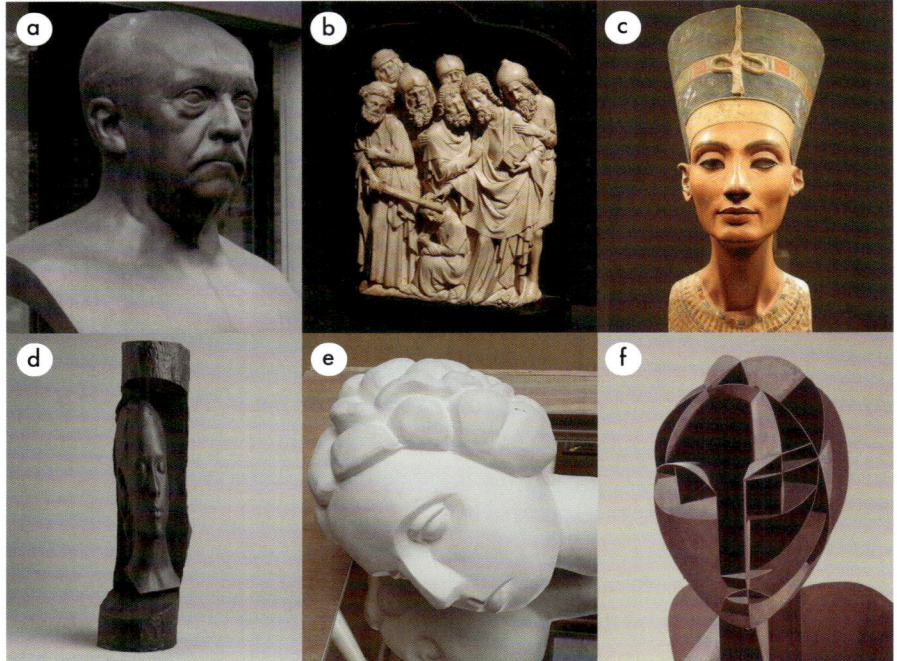

Figure 5. Images of Sculptures with Open or Closed Eyes.
(a) Adolf von Hildebrand, *Bust of Hermann von Helmholtz*, 1897.
(b) Anonymous, *The Arrest of Christ*, 1300–1324.
(c) Bust of Nefertiti.
(d) Jaume Plensa, *The Four Elements – Fire*, 2024.
(e) Tibos Chloë, buste Damya Laoui, 2023. KVAB.
(h) Head No. 2, Naum Gabo © Nina & Graham Williams/Tate, 2024.

Turning to the final triplet of associations

As mentioned before, Plensa's sculpted heads are all turned into different directions, suggesting traces between the different locations and connections to the associated surroundings. Obviously, the viewers of the sculpture will also contribute significantly to the interpretation and impact of the artwork. In this last section, I will attempt to extrapolate beyond my previous musings about what eyes and gazes can tell us – even when depicted in photographs, paintings, and sculptures, instead of being physically present in humans viewed directly.

Visual perception hinges on three key players. The *eyes* must be open and directed at something for us to see something clearly. In the early days of optics and vision, so-called extramission theories emphasized this *directionality* as if the eyes were shining light onto objects in the external world. During the Renaissance, important developments such as linear perspective in painting, improved understanding of the anatomy of the eye, and increased knowledge of the optics of lenses and the camera obscura had led to the discovery of retinal images by Kepler. This finding has also caused a great deal of misunderstanding about vision, however, such as the risk of an infinite regress implied by some higher mental entity (the homunculus) 'looking' at these retinal images to interpret them. To be sure, this way of thinking is still sometimes present in contemporary visual neuroscience focusing on how lower brain areas communicate signals to higher order brain areas or on how higher areas try to decode information in lower areas (communicating to whom? decoding for whom?). Another problem is the emphasis on inverse optics, trying to explain how the visual system can infer three-dimensional scenes from two-dimensional images, along with its associated emphasis on the veridicality of vision, assuming an entity ("The All Seeing Eye"[9]) that has direct access to the world "as it is."

In addition to the directionality of the eyes, understanding vision requires also a study of the *brain*. No less than one third of the human brain is engaged with visual processing, clearly demonstrating the role of vision in how we relate to the world. Indeed, vision has sometimes been compared to the canary in the coal mine, indexing long before cognitive or language impairments occur that something might be going wrong with the brain (e.g., psychosis, dementia, stroke, tumor). Our current understanding of the visual system has distinguished several brain areas across the four lobes (occipital, temporal, parietal, frontal), each with some level of specialization in extracting and representing specific aspects of the visual inputs (form, color, motion, and even distinct semantic categories such as faces, bodies, animals, tools, etc.). Yet, above all, the brain's enormous power and flexibility hinges on the *connectivity* and so-called communication between all these brain areas. Current artificial neural networks have approached or even exceeded standard human performance levels in dedicated tasks – such as object categorization in pictures, in addition to person and action identification in videos – by mimicking the multilayered, highly connected scanning, filtering, and abstraction operations that are supposed to take place in the human brain. Not a single artificial neural network, though – regardless of its millions of training images and high-speed processors – can even approach the spontaneous and flexible execution of all of the visual tasks we humans do with a single, unsupervised multi-purpose system, let alone all other biological and psychological functions our brains fulfill.

Last but not least, I want to emphasize the crucial aspect of *intentionality* which defines, and probably constitutes, the powers of our human *mind*. On the one hand, we have the implicit assumptions of mainstream vision science, underlying its conceptual toolbox, inherited from signal processing in linear systems engineering as well as information processing, with notions of feedforward and feedback information exchange between layers in the cortical hierarchy. On the other, I believe we need to do justice to the fact that eyes and brains are embodied; that our bodies are biological entities with an important evolutionary and developmental history; that humans live in a particular surrounding and act on it; and that we all have motivations, desires, and feelings that drive our actions. When we perceive, we do not just receive stimuli from our senses, but we are actively engaged in particular actions. Perception is in essence not the reconstruction of an objective 3D world from the images we receive but the active and subjective construction of short-lived forms of awareness, sometimes seemingly rich in detail, but always only approximations that are usually good enough for the things we need to do or even for long-term survival. Perception is essentially directed at the objects, persons, scenes, and events in our surroundings. This is also why we read so much into the eyes of a real or depicted person, even when their eyes are looking down or closed. We are not just passively registering the local features of the eye or its components, but we are imposing inter-pretations of what we have learned to be useful qualities of mental states expressed in human eyes.

I hope that everyone can now see (and understand) the enormous power of human perception. I also hope that no person continues to have their eyes wide shut, refusing to see what is in plain view, when highlighted from a phenomenological perspective instead of a reductionistic perspective on human vision.

Notes

1   Peter Mundy and Lisa Newell, "Attention, Joint Attention, and Social Cognition," *Current Directions in Psychological Science* 16, no. 5 (October 2007): 269–274, https://doi.org/10.1111/j.1467–8721.2007.00518.x.

2   Lilian R. Masek, Brianna T. M. McMillan, Sarah J. Paterson, Catherine S. Tamis-LeMonda, Roberta Michnick Golinkoff, and Kathy Hirsh-Pasek, "Where Language Meets Attention: How Contingent Interactions Promote Learning," *Developmental Review* 60 (June 2021): 100961, https://doi. org/10.1016/j.dr.2021.100961.

3   Tony Charman, "Why is Joint Attention a Pivotal Skill in Autism?," *Philosophical Transactions of the Royal Society B*, 358 (February 2003): 315–324, https://doi.org/10.1098/rstb.2002.1199.

4   Alvin I. Goldman, "Theory of Mind," in *The Oxford Handbook of Philosophy of Cognitive Science*, eds. Eric Margolis, Richard Samuels, and Stephen P. Stich (Oxford: Oxford University Press, 2012), 402–424, https://doi.org/10.1093/oxfordhb/9780195309799.013.0017.

5   Aline Verstraten, "Laying Down Colours and Covering Up Layers," *FORUM+* 30, no. 1/2 (May 2023): 64–67, https://doi.org/10.5117/FORUM2023.1/2.008.VERS.

6   Jan Koenderink and Andrea van Doorn, *Hildebrand's Vision: Art for the Eye* (Utrecht: The Clootcrans Press, 2024), 1–266.

7   Nalini Ambady and Max Weisbuch, "On Perceiving Facial Expressions: the Role of Culture and Context," in *The Oxford Handbook of Face Perception*, eds. Andrew J. Calder, Gillian Rhodes, Mark H. Johnson, and James V. Haxby (Oxford: Oxford University Press, 2011), 479–488, https://doi.org/10.1093/oxfordhb/9780199559053.013.0024.

8   Janine Willis and Alexander Todorov, "First Impressions: Making Up Your Mind After a 100-ms Exposure to a Face," *Psychological Science* 17 (July 2006): 592–598, https://doi.org/10.1111/j.1467–9280.2006.01750.x.

9   Jan Koenderink, "The All Seeing Eye? (Guest Editorial)," *Perception* 43, no. 1 (January 2014): 1–6, https://doi.org/10.1068/p4301ed.

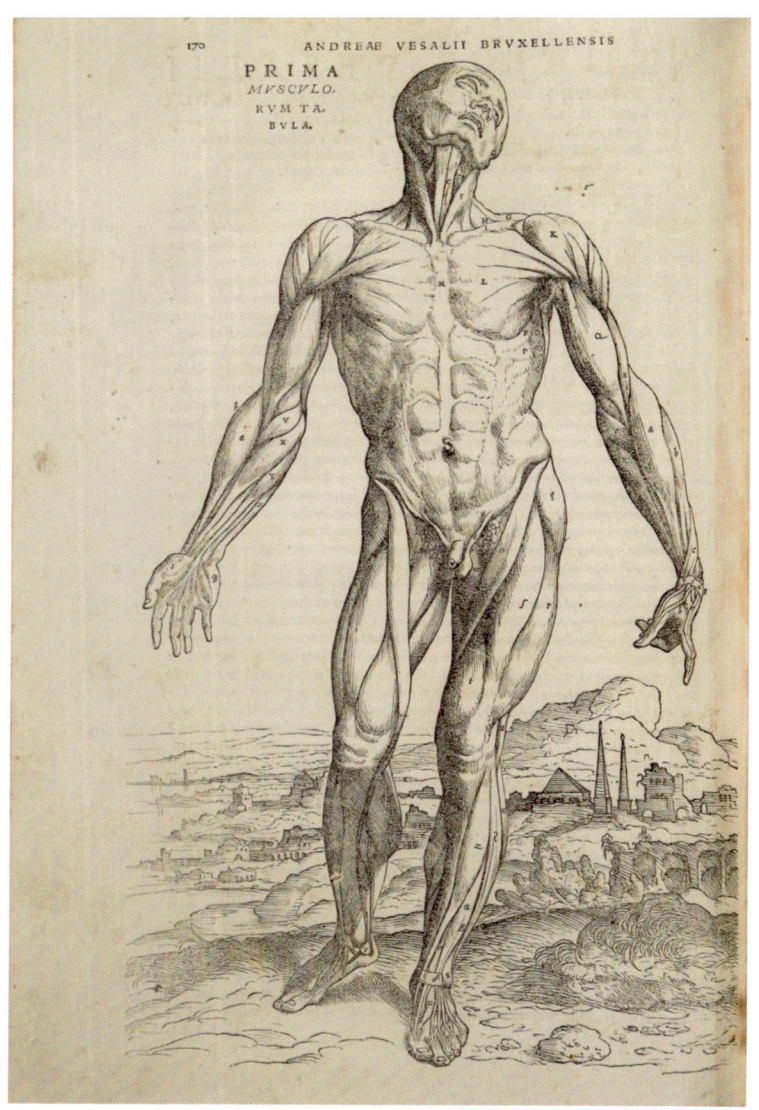

Engraving from Andreas Vesalius, *De humani corporis fabrica libri septem*.
Basel, Joannes Oporinus, 1543. p. 170. © KU Leuven Digital Lab

One Sedes Sapientiae, Two Locations, Four Elements

Mark Derez

On a wooden panel in Vienna's Kunsthistorisches Museum, Arcimboldo is playing with fire. A fuse covers the forehead of the allegorical figure, and glowing flames burst forth from their head. Here, all that glistens is gold, gold that has been tried in fire (Revelation 3:18). The torso consists of tools for war, firearms: an arquebus, a mortar shell, and an early type of musket. Around the neck hang flintstones and fire strikers, interwoven into the gold chain for the House of Habsburg's Order of the Golden Fleece. Arcimboldo's painting is part of a series with the four elements. In Leuven, Jaume Plensa takes up this cycle again on two locations: in the University Library as well as on the grounds of the university's former hospitals.

The element fire – fire in combination with the violence of war – is definitely appropriate in the University Library. The fire strikers on the Golden Fleece chain hang around the library tower; Saint Michael goes at the dragon with a flaming sword; and in a bas-relief in the top gable, flames are shooting out of the old library. It was housed in the medieval University Hall, which had acquired a baroque upper story in the seventeenth century and a separate addition for the library in the eighteenth century. In the nineteenth century, the library would well-nigh overgrow the entire Hall.

The entrance for the University Hall is still adorned above with the faintly legible motto *Sapientia aedificavit sibi domum*: "Wisdom has built herself a house" (Proverbs 9:1). Wisdom had also carved out seven pillars that were traditionally connected with the *Artes liberales*: the linguistic trivium (grammar, logic, rhetoric) and the mathematical quadrivium (arithmetic, geometry, astronomy, music). They were the Liberal Arts, the skill set providing access to the university.

Three hundred thousand books (the precipitate of the intellectual history of the Alma Mater) and a sumptuous gallery (the most exquisite library interior in the Low Countries) went up in flames in August 1914. The fire was ignited by German troops as retribution for the alleged actions of Belgian snipers. In the English press, the *Flames of Louvain* blazed high (Barbara Tuchman). There they spoke of *The Oxford of Belgium*, a designation Leuven gladly accepted for itself.

The attack on this cultural legacy aroused both indignation and solidarity worldwide. In 25 (Allied and neutral) countries, committees collected books and money for the reconstruction. The Spanish committee was led by the then duke of Alba. The American committee stole the show with the all-in-one offer of a new library building, philanthropy, and cultural diplomacy. On the Fourth of July, the "Stars and Stripes" waved from the tower. The architect Whitney Warren, known for his Grand Central Terminal in New York City, erected a nostalgic structure, amply historicizing: Flemish Renaissance on an American scale, to be sure. The style made reference to the Spanish period with the Habsburgs and Alba, though primarily and expressly to the Golden Age of Leuven's university, with humanists like Erasmus and Lipsius and, in their wake, the scientists Vesalius and Mercator.

From a distance, the profile of the University Library with its clock tower recalls the Peace Palace in The Hague, which also came about thanks to American sponsorship. Yet the University Library is at the same time a war monument as well, having the heraldic animals of the Allies on its balustrades and ramparts, as well as a madonna with a golden sword piercing a German eagle on the top gable. Revenge tastes sweet, yet bitter afterward – and definitely un-Christian. The issue of guilt remained a burning question throughout the entire period between the wars. And, as if once was not enough, the disaster of August 1914 repeated itself in May 1940, when the library was burnt to ashes yet again.

Jaume Plensa's new statue in the gallery of the University Library represents the element fire, yet does not evoke its scorching power. The large head appears serene, restrained, with eyes lowered and the whisper of a smile. It seems hidden in a hollow space, a niche, a cabinet with a canopy even, a baldachin, the start for a tabernacle. Unintentionally, the image calls forth the memory of the *Sedes Sapientiae*, the icon for Leuven par excellence. The *Sedes* is present in the library on a side gable (Jozef van Uytvanck), as well as prominently placed above the reading room entrance, opposite the foliage of an arborvitae (Jacques Moeschal), here again quite appropriately quoting and admonishing from the book of Proverbs: "Wisdom has built herself a house."

Maesta from Byzantium to Catalonia

In the visual arts, representing Mary as the *Sedes Sapientiae* (Seat of Wisdom) goes back to a very old tradition, including examples in Coptic and Byzantine church services. There, the *Sedes Sapientiae* appears as a salient feature in the iconostases that close off the public part in the church nave from the sanctuary for the altar, reserved for ministers of the Mass. Or it stands out prominently as a mosaic or fresco in the apse of early Christian basilicas. The simple Jewish girl from the Bible has in the meantime by way of theological trickery been upgraded, shall we say, to heavenly Queen. She is seated on a throne like a Byzantine empress, austerely exalted, composed, and sober in her expression. The Mother of God appears, as is said, in majesty (*en majesté*). In Duccio, Cimabue, and Giotto, she is surrounded as well by a full courtly entourage of angels and saints.

The *maesta* from the *duocento* recalls the Byzantine style, which is called hieratic because it is governed by religious rules. Within the Eastern churches, the prototype developed from the seventh century forward into a fixed model, which later also received the appellation *Sedes Sapientiae*. Mary is represented frontally, seated in a chair with Jesus on her lap, mostly in a frontal view as well. After a couple of centuries, the style found its way to the Western church, first in the art of miniature beginning in the ninth century, though not until the eleventh century in sculpture. An exquisite example – which originally came from the Meuse region and is preserved in the M(useum) Leuven – is provided by the *Sedes Sapientiae* in Leuven's Convent of the Black Sisters of Nazareth.

Jaume Plensa may know of the *Sedes Sapientiae* from the many examples in the Museo Frederic Mares in Barcelona and, of course, from the Black Madonna of the holy mountain Montserrat – the patroness of Catalonia who

53

is affectionately called *la Moreneta* (a distant cousin of the black madonna in Halle [Belgium]). Even into the 1950s, the legendary Leuven art historian Jan Karel Steppe (1918–2009) was roaming through the Pyrenees in his car, scouring deserted mountain chapels in Catalonia. He found what he was looking for everywhere. Providing for his delight were the visual representations of the the Mother of God in majesty (as the Seat of Wisdom), who was venerated as the *Gran Senora*. Back in Leuven, Professor Steppe became the authoritative advocate for the local *Gran Senora*, the *Sedes Sapientiae* in St. Peter's Church.

On her further passage in the West, the *Sedes Sapientiae* does seem to lose some of her shine and splendor. She loses height as well. In Scandinavia, the madonnas still attain almost 90 centimeters, but in the south of France, especially in the Massif Central, they do not reach beyond 70 centimeters. Sometimes they look clumsy and seem somewhat primitively carved in wood. Even so, their block-like appearance does lend them power. Sometimes it seems as if the virgin forms one single entity with the chair (the throne she sits on), and it is as if she herself forms the chair for the child (the throne for her son). What they lack in allure, the rugged sculptures gain in authenticity and spiritual radiance. Deficiencies in expression lend them a high degree of abstraction.

A new image

The static character of the *Sedes Sapientiae* from the Romanesque era became difficult to reconcile with the dynamics of the Gothic style. In it, the madonna breaks free from the block and stands up from her chair, no longer placing the child on her knee but carrying it on her arm. No longer frontal in her aspect, but *en ronde bosse* (in the round), she is more on the move and displays the typical S-shaped pose, like the Burgundian madonna on the top gable of the University Library.

In Leuven, the Gothic takes off in the fifteenth century. By establishing a university (1425), Leuven puts itself on the map again, no longer as a textiles center but as the intellectual capital of the Low Countries. In the context of this same city marketing, the town seems to deploy another tool as well: a large-scale campaign to renew the city center. The entire heart of the city is one big construction site, with its new city hall in scaffolding and

St. Peter's Church being completely restyled and receiving a new Gothic structure as well. Around 1442, the Gothic choir is consecrated. The main cult statue was also up for renewal. It was found to be too unsightly, perhaps in regard of the new architectural decor, though certainly with an eye towards the processions in which it had to be visible to the droves of people, as well as at a distance.

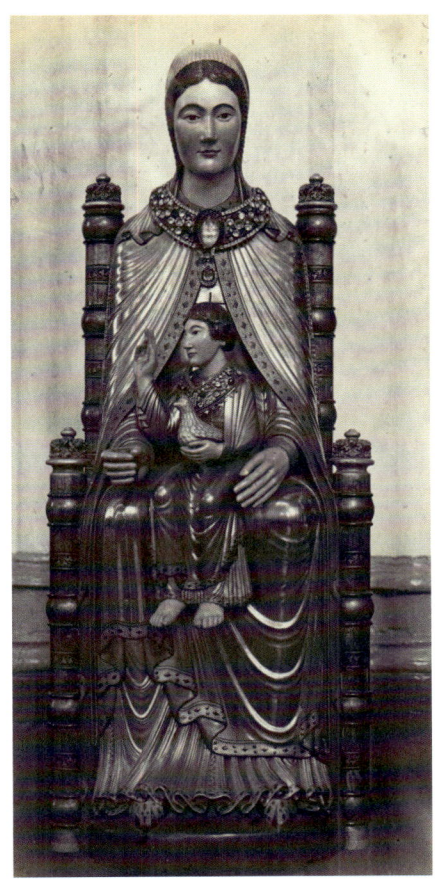 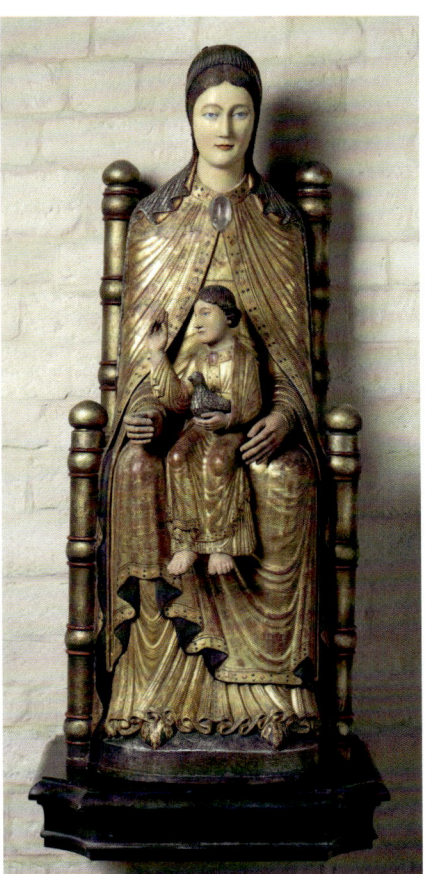

Left: *Sedes Sapientiae*. Photo by Edmond Fierlants from before 1865. KU Leuven, Universiteitsarchief © KU Leuven. Digital Lab

Right: Nicolaas de Bruyn (sculptor) and Roelof van Velpe (polychromeur), *Sedes Sapientiae*, 1442. St. Pieterskerk/M Leuven. Photo by Dominique Provost © meemoo. Art in Flanders

The commission was entrusted to Nicolaas de Bruyn. This sculptor from Brussels had finished a statue of Saint Peter for his namesake chapel at the cemetery. Shortly before, together with the cabinetmaker Gerard Goris, De Bruyn had delivered the seating for the choir – evidently to everyone's satisfaction, certainly to that of the chapter canons (usually professors from the university): they could, while standing, lean with their behinds on the pew seats with 'misericords' (supports on the bottom of those seats when turned-up). Master Nick had tricked them out with the usual drolleries: dunces, 'facemakers,' mermaids, and mythical beasts. Demons swarm among courtesans and haughty lords, who may fall prey to them at any instant. It is the late Middle Ages *au grand complet*, for edification and pleasure, even for the professors making use of the supports. Together with the cabinetmaker Arend van der Horst, Nicolaas de Bruyn was also to produce a tabernacle and a litter for the statue. De Bruyn completed the work in 1442, and for doing it took in 20 *saluts d'or* (gold pieces), of which seven came from the chapter's account and thirteen were charged to the city coffers. He was to supply the wood himself. Strangely enough, opinions in art history, so called, diverge as concerns the kind of wood: lime, oak, walnut, and also apple or pear. Limewood seems the most obvious, as it is easy to work on.

The template for the statue's polychromy might have been designed by none other than Dirk Bouts – an enticing, plausible, yet unproven hypothesis. According to that celebrated master's design, it was likely the city painter, Roelof van Velpe, who would actually carry out the painting with precious pigments. For the polychromy of the statue and pedestal as well as the litter to carry them (for the processions!), he took in 20 *saluts*, a considerable amount, just as much as the sculptor. The face, the hands, the footwear, and the narrow upturns in the clothes were painted. The garments were gilded, the veil silver-plated, just as the bird and the throne, too, had gotten touches of silver.

Spanish fashion

Just like the old one, the new sculpture was draped with a cloak from time to time. Like clockwork, it was regularly refurbished at the expense of the city magistrate. Eventually, the *Sedes Sapientiae* had a precious wardrobe (silk, damask, brocade) at her disposal. The madonna seemed to become a fashionista, certainly in the seventeenth century, when she got fitted according to the Spanish fashion with the *vertugadin*, a cone-shaped ceremonial garment that stood stiffly from all the gold thread in it. This *fardegalijn* or *verdegaal*, as it was called in Flemish, did not seem to fit the statue on the whole. No worries: for the sake of the formal cloak, the posts of the throne were thoughtlessly sawed off, one of the Virgin's hands was amputated, and the child lost out on a few finger joints. What price beauty?!

The wounded statue with the maimed throne is known to us from an as yet still unidentified lithograph in an 1842 periodical. In that year – exactly 400 years, of all things, after the statue was produced by Nicolaas de Bruyn – the sculpture was vigorously restored by the Leuven sculptor Pieter Goyers (1796–1847). The statue was stripped for good, while the original polychromy also had to go. The throne got frumpy finials in the form of inverted scroll-shaped brackets or corbels that the restorer had copied from the fifteenth-century stone sculpture on the city hall, which he was also working on at that moment. The amputated parts were replaced, and from that point on, the Virgin always had an impressive scepter pressed into her hand.

An ominous motto

The university, which was founded in its modern form in 1834 by the Belgian bishops, was immediately dedicated to the Holy Virgin. At the celebration of the 75th anniversary of that confessional institution in 1909, a new neo-gothic seal was brought into use with the *Sedes Sapientiae* as its central image. A new tradition caught on.

The *Sedes Sapientiae* stands out as perfectly sovereign on the vignettes pasted into books from when the University Library was rebuilt after World War I. These were *ex dono* bookplates for the donations that poured in from neutral and Allied countries, as well as *ex libris* plates for the learning materials that Germany had to restitute in executing Article 47 of the Treaty of Versailles (*ouvrage restitué par l'Allemagne*). On the vignette designed by the Leuven art historian Raymond Lemaire (1878–1954), the representation of the *Sedes* was dramatically affixed, including flickering flames – the *Flames of Louvain* that had evoked Leuven's libricide since 1914. The tragic memory was compensated for by an optimistic emblematic device in the lettering along the margins: *Sedes Sapientiae non evertetur*, the seat of wisdom shall not be overthrown. Even so, the purposeful slogan also had something ominous to it, as if one wanted to dare fate. Indeed, it proved to turn out that way. The irony, tragically, was that of the 900,000 books given this hopeful motto, scarcely a few tens of thousands or so were left after the second burning of the University Library in May 1940.

Halfway through the 1920s, the university suddenly appeared to realize that it was, in retrospect, actually five centuries old. Paradoxically enough, the amnesia seemed just to have lifted as the result of the trauma of the war, but it could also have a favorable outcome with the fundraising for the reconstruction – certainly with Americans, who are so keen on tradition and history. Between the wars, the heyday of a profuse Catholicism also dawned. Glory days for the *Sedes Sapientiae* kicked off now, too. In 1927, amid the festive mood surrounding the university's 5th centenary, the *Sedes* was ceremoniously crowned by the cardinal-archbishop of Mechelen. The new crown and necklaces were gifted by the university. The actual ceremony was preceded by a traditional triduum, a religious observance lasting three days, concluded in a song of praise with lyrics by Jozef Simons (1888–1948) and 500 performers outdoors on the Oude Markt square. That much Catholic triumphalism was, of course, a boost for the Catholic part of the population, as well as a clerical statement in a largely anti-clerical town. And, without a doubt, the *Sedes Sapientiae* experienced her finest hour.

It is unnecessary to mention that these sorts of religious exercises were also connected with indulgences, including profitable discounts for the period after death to be spent in purgatory, and those credits could run quite high. Ever since Luther, this sales scheme had been exposed to the sharpest criticism, though the practice was still fully in force in the twentieth century. According to the university's yearbook (*Annuaire de l'Université catholique de Louvain*, 1844), 300 days worth of indulgence were associated with a prayer to the *Sedes Sapientiae*.

And then World War II broke out. Reportedly, students were kneeling before her throne at all hours of the day, and in keeping with their gender, the female students brought her bunches of flowers in an uninterrupted homage. During the frightening hours of 1943–1944, the entire academic community of professors and students came together every evening to pray the rosary – that is, until in the night from May 11 to 12, 1944, when the Allies undertook an aerial bombardment directed at a crucial line of communications for the

German army. One bomb struck the north transept of St. Peter's Church, and the *Sedes Sapientiae* got buried under the marble of her own altar. Still, the pious motto *Sedes Sapientiae non evertetur* turned out to be true, after all. The heavily hit university did not get wiped out, and the crushed statue could be restored, with the patience of an angel, by the sculptor Jozef van Uytvanck (1884–1967). The posts of the throne acquired their familiar spherical finials.

The emblematic device in Latin which had been so anchored in the tragic history of both world wars was pulled out once more in a much more prosaic context, namely, that of Belgium's language battle during the 1960s. *Sedes Sapientiae non evertetur* became the slogan for the conservative circles that resisted splitting up Leuven's university into two autonomous institutions and transferring the French-language university to a brand new city campus in the Wallonian part of the country (Louvain-la-Neuve). Into the dispute came the regionalization of the country and the emancipation of Flanders, as well as the democratization of education. In 1968, the split was a fact. Evidently, though, the *Sedes Sapientiae* did not allow itself to be politically manipulated. The statue of the *Sedes* stayed on its familiar spot in old Leuven (Louvain-la-Veuve). Yet the logo continued to be used as a certification mark (CE) by the Dutch- as well as French-language universities. That common usage successfully conveys the corporate identity of both sister institutions. It is not the image for the image's sake, as the eighteenth-century pilgrim letter reminds us. It is about the spirit that the Academy radiates.

Andreas Vesalius

The second location that Jaume Plensa has selected for his Leuven project lies completely at the edge of the historical inner city, along its thirteenth-century wall. The wall possesses a conspicuous texture with alternating white and brown rows of (ferrous) sandstone. On one of the towers, an eighteenth-century pavilion has been erected. Behind it runs the Dyle River. A century ago, when Leuven students were in thrall with the Heidelberg-*Romantik*, Leuven was even called the Heidelberg on the Dyle. Yet although the Dyle may be the most rapidly flowing river in the Scheldt basin, only the discharge from Leuven's beertaps recalls that of the majestic river that is Heidelberg's Neckar. Located nearby was the Brewery School – an academic discipline that was indispensable in a town where the scent of malt is never out of the air. Here, incidentally, the Dyle has been entirely covered over – not because bikes are regularly thrown into it (and in one novel even bishops), but for sanitary reasons. For this site is also the grounds of the former hospitals and is entirely dominated by the practice and science of medicine.

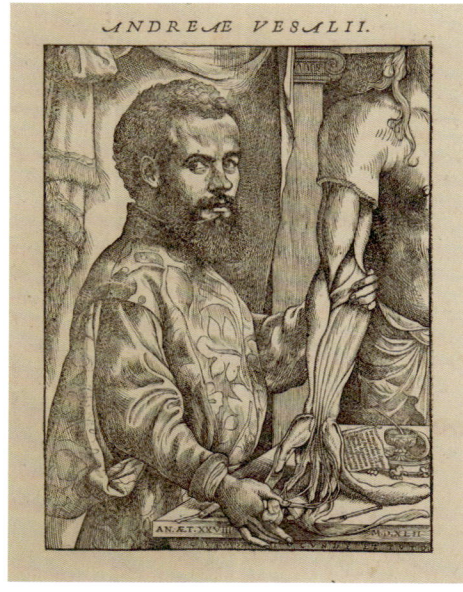

Engraving from Andreas Vesalius, *De humani corporis fabrica libri septem*. Basel, Joannes Oporinus, 1543 [KU Leuven Digital Lab]

Andreas Vesalius (1514–1564) is the celebrity who gave his name to a succession of institutes. Vesalius himself was an alumnus of the Collegium Trilingue, Erasmus's 'College of Three Languages.' Without Erasmus, no Vesalius: textual criticism undermined the argument for the authority of the old masters. Scientists ought not rely on superannuated commentaries, but autonomously take the object of research itself as their point of departure. The catalyst for this scientific humanism was the mathematician Gemma Frisius (1508–1555). To this very day, his students are the object of national pride: the geographer Gerard Mercator (1512–1594), the botanist Rembert Dodoens (1517–1585), and the anatomist Andreas Vesalius. With their 'atlases' they mapped out the world, the plant kingdom, and the human body.

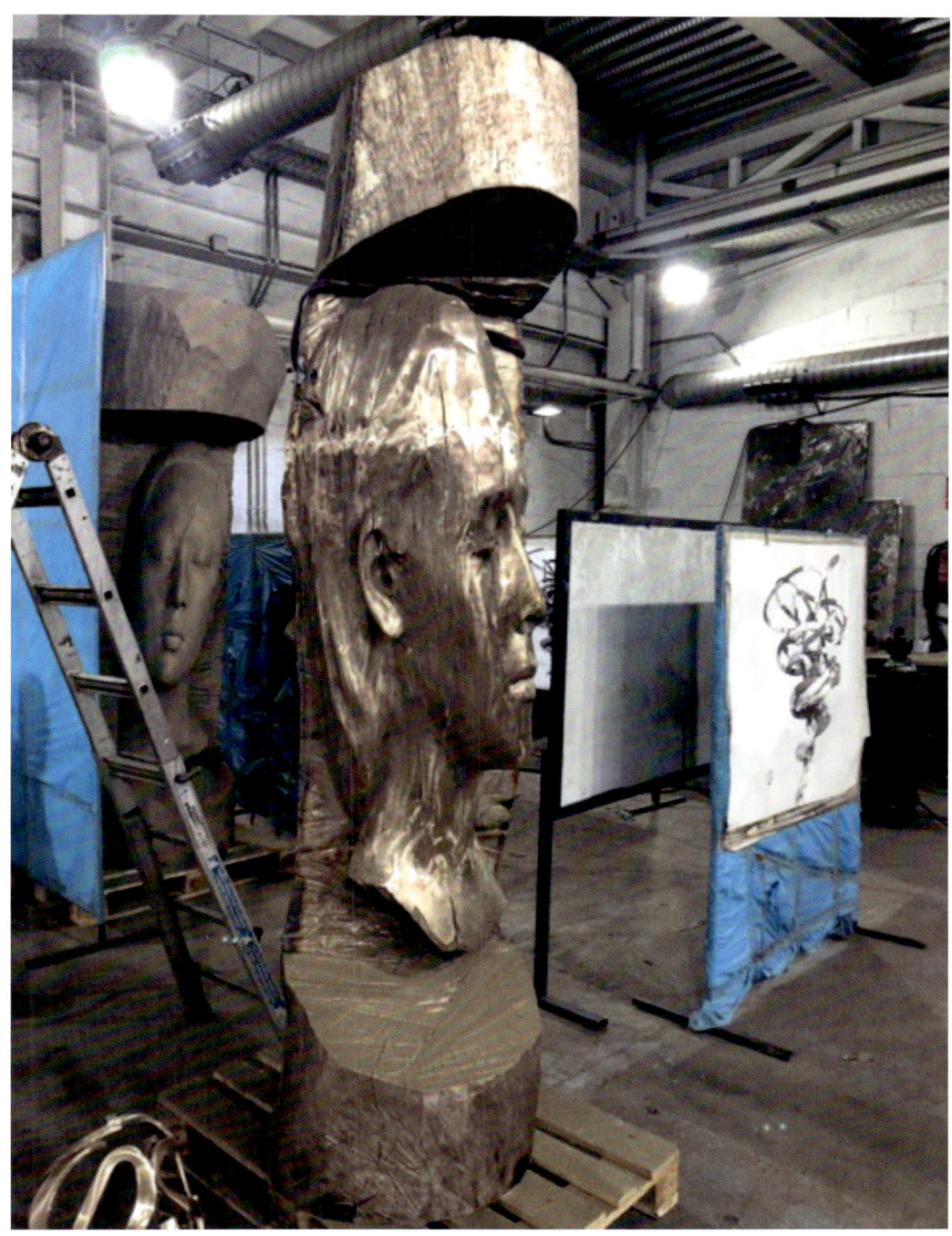

Foundry of *The Four Elements*. © Plensa Studio Barcelona

As a student, Vesalius stole corpses from the gallows and with his public dissections brought Leuven to the peak of anatomical education. Those who had learned to overturn texts did not recoil from opening up bodies with their own hands. Vesalius put the results of all that cutting into book form in *De humani corporis fabrica libri septem* (1549), seven volumes about the structure of the human body. With this anatomical atlas, Vesalius was a pioneer, as it were, in medical imaging. He dedicated his monumental work to Emperor Charles V, for whom Vesalius was the personal physician. Charles later gave back his personal copy to Leuven University, where it went up in flames during the burning of the library in 1914. Very recently, in early 2024, the University Library was able to lay its hands on the second edition of the *Fabrica* (1555), including corrections and conjectures, as well as notes from the hand of the master himself. The woodcuts are of an astonishing quality. The theatrical poses of the models do not in any way detract from the scientific precision of the representation.

The skeletons and muscled men call to mind Gunther von Hagen's controversial Body Worlds exhibition. And the stringy men who represent the circulatory and nervous systems look quite a lot like some of the figures constructed of metal wire by Jaume Plensa himself. With his *Fabrica*, Vesalius wanted to instruct and inspire scientists and artists alike: art and science, both in pursuit of finding the truth. Plensa's totem is a tribute to that search.

A yellow elephant

A hundred years after Vesalius, the Faculty of Medicine in Leuven received permission to build a *magnifieck Theatrum Anatomicum*, granted by privilege on February 1, 1661. Eighty years later, around 1745, the amphitheater could finally be dedicated. It was an exceptional building that scarcely knew its equal: a completely freestanding pavilion with an octagonal central structure under a cupola and mansard roof. Together with the *hortus* – the Faculty's botanical garden (*c.* 1720) – and the chemistry laboratory (1685), the anatomical theater in the backyard of the municipal hospital formed a genuine medical campus that was entirely geared toward instruction by demonstration.

Around 1765, Laurent-Benoît Dewez (1731–1812) was tasked with a neoclassical reconstruction of the orangery. The court architect designed a monumental entrance gate as well, at the insistence, too, of the prestigious University Press, which was also housed there and took no pleasure in having a rickety fence. In 1819, the *hortus* was found to be too small (half a hectare), and it was moved to the other side of the Voer River where yet another court architect, Charles van der Straeten (1771–1834), erected an elegant orangery in an even sterner neoclassical style with Palladian motifs.

At that time, the *hortus* and the theater formed only the embryo of the future hospital complex that would develop tumultuously in the nineteenth and twentieth centuries. It began in 1838, with the construction of the pavilions for the new St. Peter's Hospital by the architect Alexander van Arenbergh (1824–1865). In 1870, Professor Joris Helleputte (1852–1925) constructed a larger anatomical theater in the neo-Gothic style – the characteristic, very rational 'engineer's Gothic,' for which he was the trailblazer. The sculptor Constantin Meunier then established his studio in the old theater (1887–1895). Another of the university's in-house architects, Vincent Lenertz (1864–1914) – also the designer of the emblem with the *Sedes Sapientiae* – took on the construction of the Pathology Institute in 1906.

Between the wars came the development of St. Raphaël's Hospital, eventually a genuine jumble of buildings, including the Cancer Institute (among others), which looks luxurious yet is not any milestone in architectural history. After World War II, St. Peter's Hospital got a colossal addition thirteen stories high, which cast its shadow over the age-old medieval hospital. In the shortest amount of time, this high-rise – the "yellow elephant" – became a bone of contention for those who had any feeling for the finely knit maze of the historical inner city. Running between the largely Dutch-language St. Raphaël's Hospital and the predominantly French-language St. Peter's Hospital, the as yet not covered Dyle River functioned as a sort of natural linguistic border in the 1950s. Afterward, the French-language Faculty of Medicine departed for Brussels, and the Dutch-language Faculty moved to the Gasthuisberg district outside the city. This spot that was so historically rich remained behind, like an orphan.

shadows

The length of each curtain
is variable following the
spirit of each poem. ~

From terrain vague to hot spot

The overall picture that emerged was that of a *terrain vague*, a waste-land, sown with archaeological relicts. There are still remnants of the nineteenth-century St. Peter's Hospital with its language of classic forms, rising up like ancient fragments high above the ground level. The passage-way by court architects and university in-house architects elsewhere on the grounds was no longer immediately legible from the wounded state of many of the structures.

Yet what had threatened to become an urban cancer will be redeveloped. To that end, the city (the municipal administration) and the university have joined hands and engaged a real estate agent. Heritage and real estate are at odds. Often heritage stands in the way (the School of Nursing had to go), but real estate can also derive added value from the heritage nearby. The protected buildings will be upgraded. The "yellow elephant" of St. Peter's Hospital has been torn down in the meantime (2019–2021), which was a considerably complicated process. The Dyle River will be uncovered again to become a blue ribbon in a green environment.

On either side of the hospital grounds there will be two attractions, a theater and a museum, though they may not be called that. The breach in the façade of the Brusselsestraat side will be closed off again by build-ing a performing arts hall designed by the London firm of Sergison Bates Architects. On the road called Minderbroedersstraat, the nineteenth-century anatomical theater will be redesigned as a *belevingscentrum* (experience center) for scientific research and social wellness. The ostensibly unique *Theatrum Anatomicum* has no chance of winning, for the entire site is now well on its way from being a *terrain vague* to becoming a *hot spot*. Jaume Plensa's totem can become its landmark.

Acknowledgements

With thanks to Soetkin Vanhauwaert, Anne Verbrugge, Norbert Moermans and Katharina Smeyers

Literature cited

Carpreau, Peter with Marjan Debaene, Ko Goubert, Goedele Pulinx and Eline Sciot. *M Collecties Beeldhouwkunst.* Leuven: M-Museum Leuven, 2014.

Coppens, Chris, Mark Derez, and Jan Roegiers, eds. *Leuven University Library, 1425–2000:* Sapientia aedificavit sibi domum. Leuven: Leuven Univ. Press, 2005.

Delbeke, Maarten, Lise Constant, and Lobke Geurs. "The Architecture of Miracle-Working Statues in the Southern Netherlands." *Revue d'histoire des religions* 232, no. 2 (2015): 211–256.

Huybens, Gilbert, David Mellaerts, and Brecht Dewilde, eds. *De Sint-Pieterskerk te Leuven. Geschiedenis, architectuur en patrimonium.* Leuven: Peeters, 2022.

Landtsheer, Jeanine de. "*Justi Lipsi Diva Lovaniensis*: An Unknown Treatise on Louvain's *Sedes Sapientiae.*" *Revue d'Histoire Ecclésiastique* 92 (1997): 135–142.

Maunder, Chris (ed.). *The Oxford Handbook of Mary.* Oxford: Oxford Univ. Press, 2019.

Snaet, Joris. "Het Anatomisch Theater." In Ex abundantia cordis: *Vriendenboek Mark Derez*, edited by Kjell Corens, Jan De Maeyer, Marc Nelissen, Nathalie Poot, Marleen Reynders, Sophie de Smet, Geert Vanpaemel, and Anne Verbrugge, 46–47. Leuven: Leuven Univ. Press, 2019.

Steppe, Jan Karel. "Madonnabeelden." *Streven* 7 (1953–1954): 101–104.

Steppe, Jan Karel. "*Sedes Sapientiae.*" In *Erasmus en Leuven*, edited by Jan Roegiers and J. K. Steppe, 74–75. Leuven: [s.n.], 1969. Exhibition catalog.

Van der Essen, Leon. *Notre-Dame de St. Pierre (Louvain). « Siège de la Sagesse » (1129–1927).* Leuven: Peeters, 1927.

Vanpaemel, Geert, Mark Derez, and Jo Tollebeek, eds. *Album of a Scientific World. The University of Louvain around 1900*. Leuven: Leuven Univ. Press, 2012.

Vanpaemel, Geert, ed. *Vesalius. Het lichaam in beeld*. Leuven: Davidsfonds, 2014. Exhibition catalog.

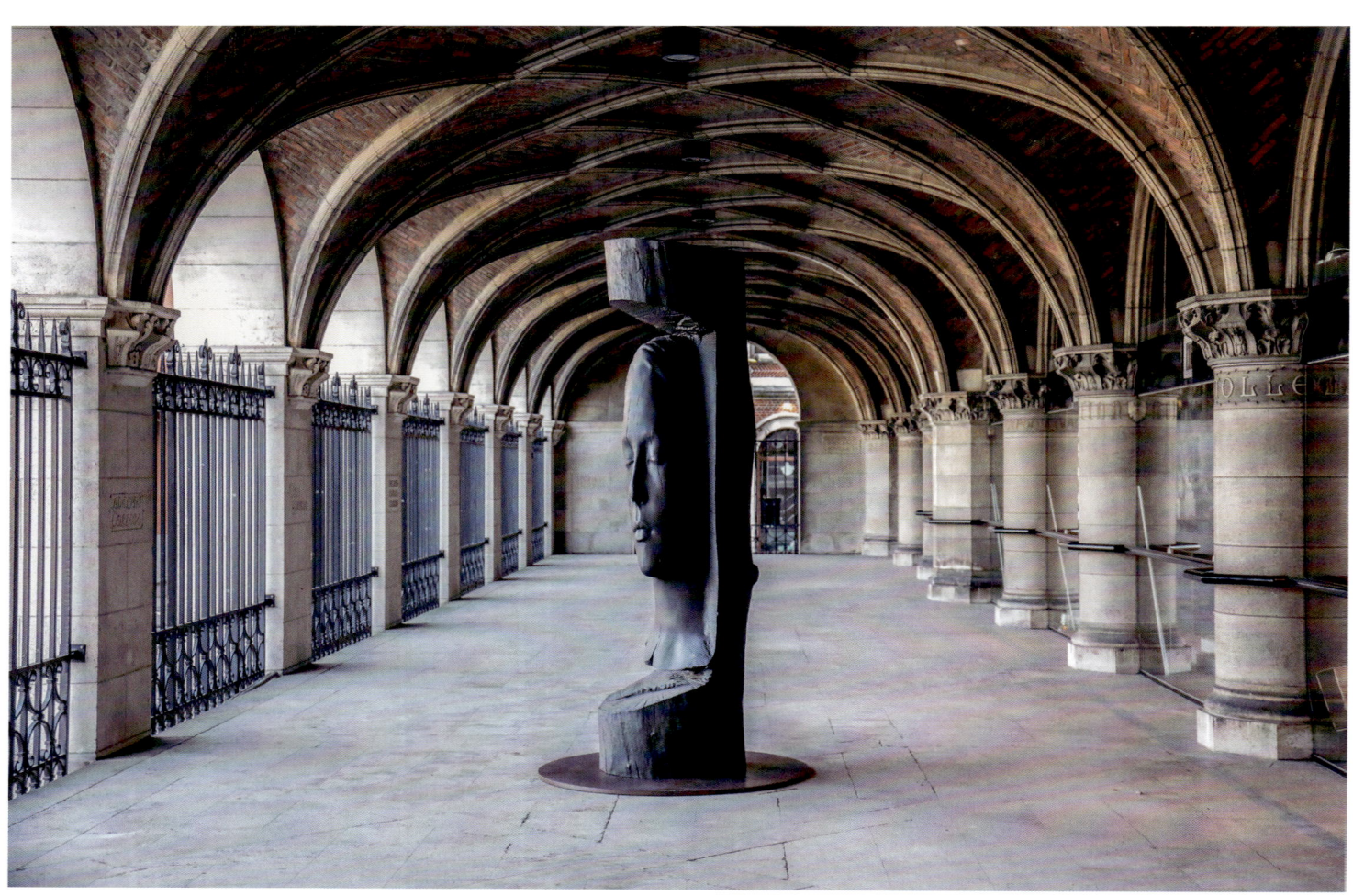

Four Elements of Academic and Artistic Research

Erik Thys

1. Earth

Since their genesis, human beings have been occupied with art and philosophy. They have been engaged in this way for much longer than these concepts have been designated and defined, let alone strictly distinguished from each other. The American philosopher Alva Noë describes art and philosophy as "strange tools."[1] He characterizes them as those things that humans just do, and which go just a bit further than what is merely utilitarian. An example is human breastfeeding. It is a more laborious process than for other mammals, and only in human communities are there all manner of activities coupled to it out of necessity. This behavioral pattern reaches beyond mere feeding for both the baby and the mother: the baby grabs, chews, and bites, falls asleep and cries, while the mother supports, guides, and cradles the baby, as well as speaks and interacts with them. In this way, a biological function becomes a complex, ordered ritual forming the basis for thinking that organizes. Ultimately, what sprouts from this germ is what we today call art and philosophy.

69

According to Noë, these tools are of course for contemplating the ways in which our lives are structured and ordered, and which allow us to gain more insight into who we are, what we are, and why we are. According to Noë, art and philosophy are therefore in the first place instruments for a kind of self-investigation. He calls them "strange" tools because in a second phase, as a result of this investigating, they structure and order our lives anew. You could say that in this way art and philosophy have a recursive aspect, for they are instruments that not only research but also change reality, a new reality that subsequently can be investigated again, in an endless succession. It takes, in our view, little effort to add science to this sequence of "strange tools" and, in so doing, arrive at the three major domains of human investigation and creation: art, science, and philosophy. If all this is correct, then we are dealing with three branches that grew from the same trunk, rooted in the earth of human biology. The branches are strongly connected with human action, with praxis. You could say that praxis, investigation, and creation in humans are connected with one another, as in Heidegger's hammer. After all, a hammer can be taken "ready-to-hand" (*zuhanden*) as an instrument for an activity, but it can also be "present-at-hand" (*vorhanden*) as an object for observation.[2] In Heidegger, the step toward observation is triggered as a result of a problem on the level of praxis (when, for example, the hammer is broken); though we maintain, in any event, that humans in general do not need many problems in order to reflect and to nurture creatively. With a measure of good will, one can also recognize in this process Hannah Arendt's sequence of labor (the biological function), work (the production of things), and action (taking initiative in the community).[3]

2. Water

This model for a history of their genesis can help to clarify the relation and overlap between art, science, and philosophy. In this way, for example, there is much knowledge, technology, and science hidden away in art. Take, for example, the series of sculptures with enlarged and extended women's heads by the artist Jaume Plensa. The starting point for a sculpture of this sort is generally a digital 3D model of its subject, for the most part a real person. With the aid of computer programs, the artist modifies the models by elongating them along the vertical axis and narrowing them along the

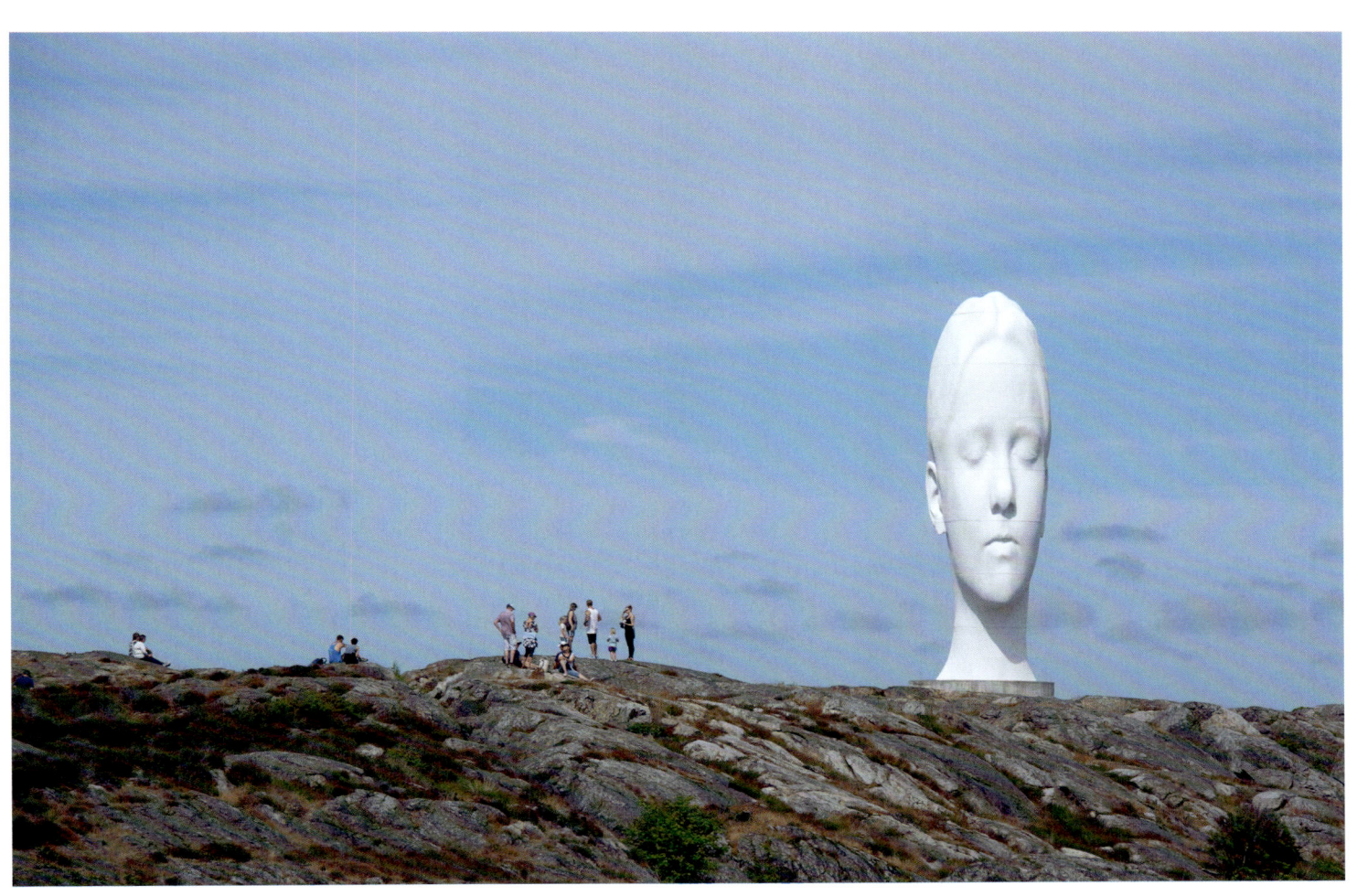

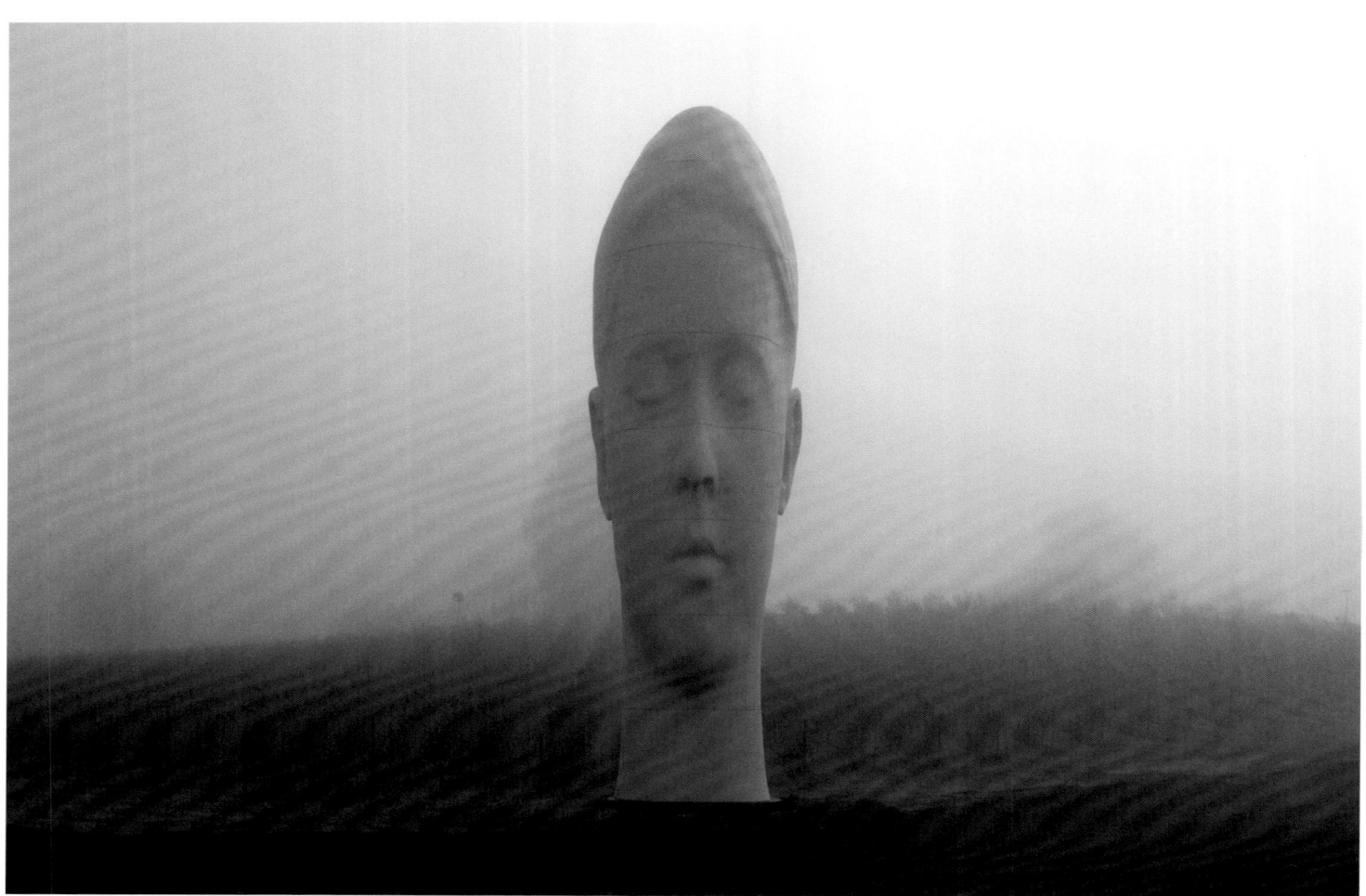

horizontal axis. Subsequently, he abstracts and changes their facial features for the "journalistic sense of the portrait to become an icon."[4] With the aid of an industrial prototyping device, he then fabricates a plastic foam model to scale, which he models by hand. The artist repeats this process many times before he produces the sculpture in its actual size. Notably: it not only involves narrowing, enlarging, and idealizing the model, as one might think at first glance. For large-scale sculptures many meters high, the artist must also take the distortion of perspective into account, meaning that we will perceive the top of a large image as smaller when we look at it from below. With large objects like trees and buildings, our perception is used to it, but not for human heads whereby we would perceive a proportionally enlarged, meters-high head as distorted. This sort of optical distortion is, to a certain extent, recognizable in the *mo'ai*, the well-known monolithic statues on Easter Island, which seen from below seem to have a disproportionally prominent chin and an especially small forehead. This is not the case in Plensa's sculptures, because he corrects the giant heads by making them progressively higher, wider, and deeper towards the top.[5] It is a technique we could compare to the *entasis* of the architects from antiquity, who corrected the geometric form of buildings for the optical distortions of the human eye. Michelangelo, too, probably intended this effect when he gave his masterpiece David a conspicuously large head and hands, so that the gigantic statue on the roof of the Duomo (the originally planned location) would come across as harmonious from the ground level.

In addition to a core artistic idea and an artisan's dexterity built on praxis, then, computer science, knowledge about materials, and awareness of optics also underlie Plensa's giant heads. Yet insight from the neurosciences also lies in this work: the narrow giant heads have a strong emotional impact, not only as a result of the ideal beauty and sacred peace they radiate, but also as a result of the distortions described above. These deviations disrupt our perception of the human head, an object for which our extreme familiarity shifts now toward surprise and strangeness. The statues confuse, seem simultaneously unreal and hyperrealistic, as an optical illusion that does not let go of us, fascinating us and compelling our contemplation. As a result of this strangeness, the sculpture acquires what neuroscientists call "salience," the "conspicuousness" of things that direct our attention, our thought, and our action. In the perception of Plensa's art, as a result, a philosophical dimension germinates as well, as in Heidegger's example of the hammer. In Plensa's sculpture, the human head so familiar to us – the object with which we probably interact the most – can no longer be taken to be harmlessly "ready-to-hand," but becomes instead "present-at-hand," as a puzzle that appeals to us and makes us reflect. The scale, the proportions, and the distortions constitute in the process the "problem" or the "strange tool" that sets reflection in motion.

In this view of things, art, science, philosophy, research, and praxis flow together like water, into a self-evident, natural stream.

3. Fire

This harmonious, idealistic narrative, however, stands in stark contrast to what today is not even called a debate any longer, but a combat: one between artistic and academic research.[6] The account of a combat traditionally begins with the introduction of the opponents in the ring, but in this case, that is where the difficulties already begin. Let us make an attempt anyway. In the one corner: academic research. What is that? The definitions are not unequivocal, but a number of elements recur: it involves investigation that is accurate, systematic, and rigorous, the function of which is to discover new knowledge and insights. Precisely because it is new, this knowledge is by definition yet undetermined and cannot be conceived as too utilitarian: it involves more than the solution of a delimited, concrete problem. This characterization becomes clear in the witticism of the rocket scientist Wernher von Braun: "Basic research is what I am doing when I don't know what I am doing." A core property of academic research lies finally in the term itself: it is research that takes place in the context of an academic institute, and which, as a result, is inscribed into a network of research by peers.

Now then, in the other corner: artistic research, which proves to be more difficult to define, even though the concept seems to be of a more recent date. More specifically, June 19, 1999, when 29 European ministers of education signed the Bologna Process, an initial declaration about creating a European space for higher education. This declaration made possible the doctoral degree in the arts, the crown on the work of academizing the arts. Academization sounds somewhat unusual here, because we already intuitively associate the word "academy" on its own with the arts, whereas originally it actually refers to philosophy, to the school of Plato. In other words, the

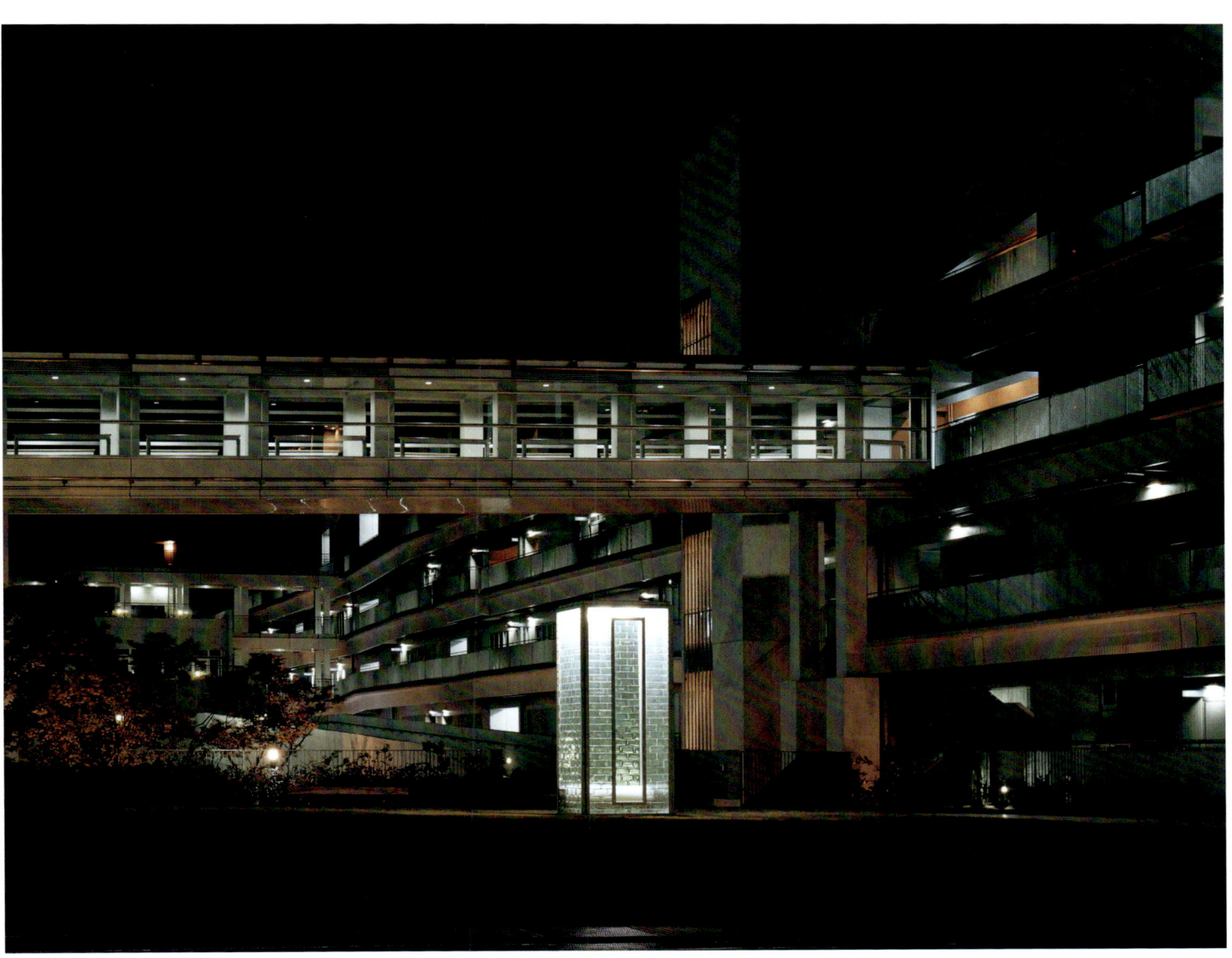

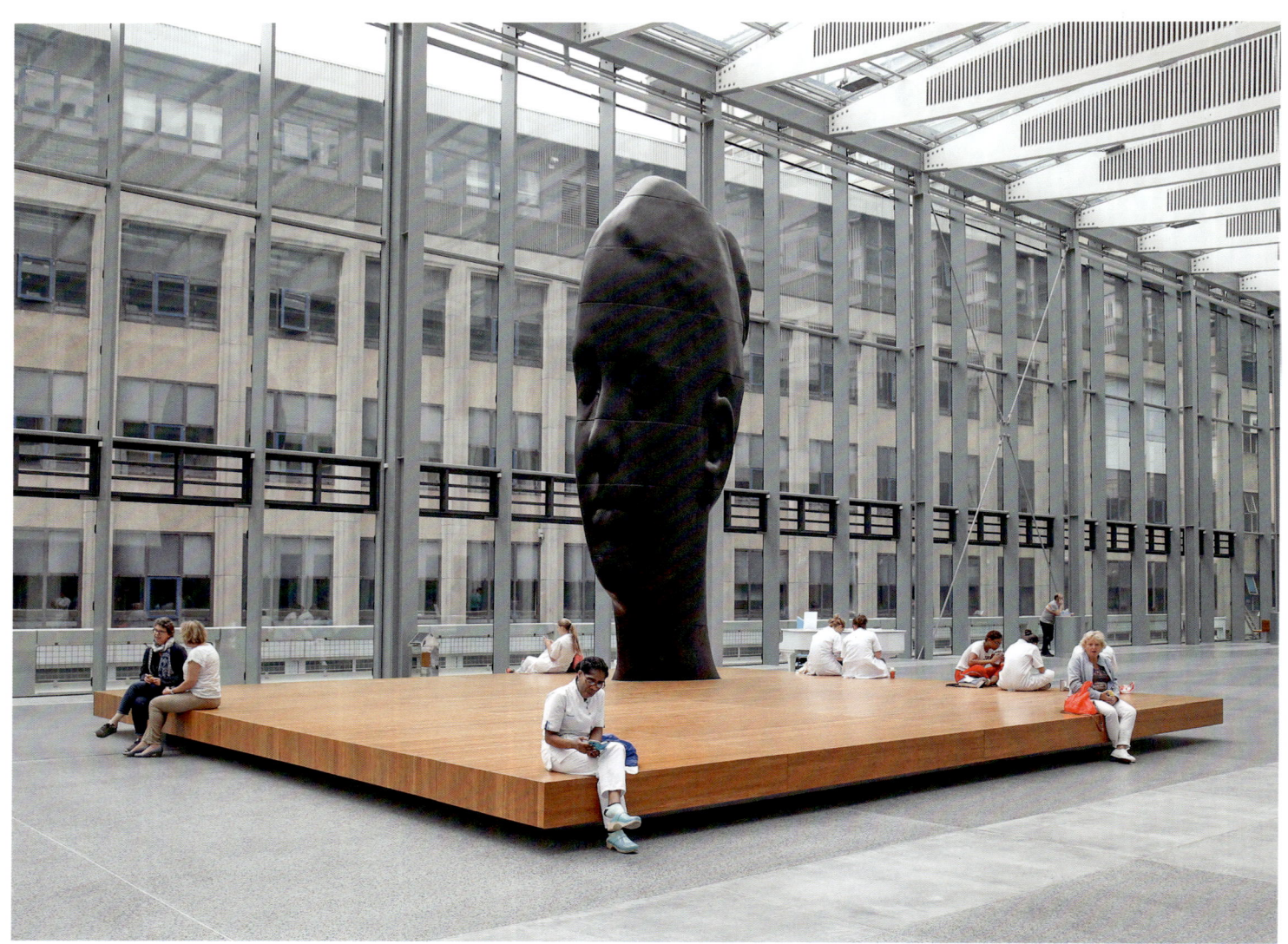

trinity of human creation – art, science, and philosophy – is rooted in the genealogy of this word. Understood, to be sure, that artistic research as such has existed much longer than the Bologna Process of course; it can even be seen as an essential component of modern art from the beginning of the twentieth century forward. The word "new" in the definition of research above is perhaps the key to this evolution. In the previous turn of the century's pivotal moment, after all, a striving, even a necessity for continuous innovation arose, compelling artists to think up new solutions for each work. Artists sought innovation not only within art but also for the concept of art itself. One could say that the cognitive aspect of art at the beginning of the twentieth century came forcefully to the fore, to the detriment of more emotional and cultural values like beauty and taste.

Upon closer inspection, it is the period in which the scientific world, too, opted for accurate, systematic, and rigorous investigation. Take 1905, the year in which Freud published his *Three Essays on the Theory of Sexuality*. These innovative and influential observations about the development of human sexuality are a model exercise in nineteenth-century science: contemplating in essayistic terms, constructing hypotheses that are theoretically consistent but not empirically tested. In the same year, Einstein published four articles, including his groundbreaking publication about the special theory of relativity. This theory is based on empirical data that unexpectedly demonstrated the immutability of the speed of light and cried out for a clarification. In the meantime, Einstein's theory has been proven experimentally countless times – typically twentieth-century science. Sciences like physics, then, are also quite appropriate for calling into question the *flou artistique* (artistic blur, or soft focus) of artistic research.

Even so, the combat has been engaged on various fronts. Voices in the art world reproach the art academies and universities, which are supposed to direct and judge artistic research, for wrongly seeing it as a new domain that they can tear into, even take over, with their scientific methods. They fear that artistic research is being subordinated to scientific systems of investigation, only still considered as a form of knowledge if it satisfies scientific norms.[7] Even sharper critique makes a connection between the scientific approach and the power structures of capitalistic society. According to these critics, behind the homogenization – the *Gleichschaltung* (cooptation) – of research lies a process of hegemonization. What is the art world to do in this light? Some go so far as to put forward a radical version of artistic research against the utilitarian knowledge of the neoliberal knowledge-based society, namely, performative, non-cognitive acts. This kind of artistic investigation generates a sort of "non-knowledge" and in so doing creates space for an epistemology that stands apart from the dominant powers-that-be.[8]

In the academic world, then again, some argue that artistic research – as that is being implemented in arts doctorates in terms of method, evaluation criteria, and presentation – has to be subjected to comparable scientific standards. They still want to preserve some space for a few of the more creative and intuitive aspects of artistic research, though in no event may artistic *praxis* pass for artistic research. And certainly not by replacing the word "praxis" with "research" in writings. Others see in this scientification the threat that a return on investment will be required in exchange for financing artistic research, by way of the valorization of artistic output – in other words, through the marketing of artworks.[8] In the fiery heat of the battle, everything is called into question over time: the meaning of research, the status of praxis, and the position of the artist/researcher. It does not help that the terms "research" and "praxis," "academic" and "scientific" are used interchangeably. Neither does the fact that the political dimensions of the conflict are simplified into an opposition between left and right, the ultimate schematizing and diabolizing of the "enemy."

Perhaps, though, the real enemy is precisely this polarization of the debate. Perhaps some connection is still conceivable. To begin with, as sketched above, there is the more or less parallel paradigm shift within modern art and modern science. A century ago, there was something in the air that was captured by both. Secondly, art and science also have surprisingly much in common in the way in which they are accepted nowadays within the field and by the wider society. Often, the valuation of art is experienced as subjective and that of science as objective. After all, a scientific publication is tested on its sound data and method, which is much less the case in the appreciation of artworks. Yet in both cases, the end stage is a form of peer review: in the end, experts in science and art pass a personal judgment about the work, which is de facto subjective in part, after which the work is able to find its way via other knowledge-based institutions such as universities, museums, galleries, conferences, journals, and so forth.

These processes, then, have more in common – and are more subjective than we think. What is more, rigorous, empirical science today is confronted with the so-called replication crisis. A decade ago, it turned out that reproducing research in psychology was much less successful than thought: researchers did not manage to achieve the same results in a control investigation as in the original investigation. Later there also proved to be problems in replicating investigations in medicine, chemistry, biology, and ... physics. Ironically enough, the causes are, among other things, psychological factors like confirmation bias and publication pressure, which scientists are vulnerable to. This crisis does not have to undermine the credibility of science per se, yet it does bring a certain relativization into the debate. Conversely, artistic research is able to benefit from empirical/scientific experience. In the way scientific research is valorized and, as the case may be, falsified within a network of experts, so, too, is artistic research best conceived in a context of experts and peers in order to acquire wider significance. Solipsistic artistic research runs the risk of devolving into outsider research. As such, it can be valuable and innovative to enter into very eccentric terrain for research, but a minimum of connection with peers is necessary for the relevance of the investigation. In the words of the Dutch author Jeroen Brouwers: "Nothing exists that does not touch something else."[9] Sometimes outsiders are discovered and overtaken later by their peers, but that is not infrequently posthumously.[10] Connection is certainly important for doctoral research in the arts. Perhaps such an investigation is still too often exclusively about researchers' own praxis and oeuvre without fully situating and connecting them in their field. The compulsion of what is new ought not lead to a landscape of ivory towers. With all respect for what is proprietary in artistic research and the central importance of the artist/researcher's praxis and personality, you could say that a doctorate still also has a social dimension. Perhaps the following citation from Heidegger applies as well to artistic research: "[T]he more unconditionally science and the man of research take seriously the modern form of their essence, the more unequivocally and the more immediately will they be able to offer themselves for the common good, and the more unreservedly too will they have to return to the public anonymity of all work useful to society."[11]

4. Air

Perhaps, though, the battle between artistic and scientific research distracts us meanwhile from a potential, common enemy: the overly strong bureaucratization of research. In the Middle Ages, students and teachers in the arts and sciences journeyed freely throughout Europe to learn and to teach. Since then, various regulations in various European countries have made this travel increasingly more difficult. A diploma in the one country was no longer valid in the other. The Bologna Process came about in order to make this free circulation of knowledge possible again and has succeeded for the most part in doing so. One necessary evil, though, was the standardization and (over-)regulation of education, along with – perhaps even more crucially – the installation of an expanded administrative apparatus for setting everything up. This bureaucratization also reached into the surrounding institutions that have to offer this standardized instruction: the universities and the academies. An organizational structure of this sort demands a stern, strongly staffed management that – in view of the age-old pronounced hierarchical structure of universities and other educational institutions – is constructed vertically and pyramidally. What emerges is a structure that is unwieldy and barely maneuverable and, as a result, can be inclined to conservatism, rigidity, and monoculture, which stands in essence at odds with innovative research. As a result, the organization also becomes more and more directed toward itself, toward its own organizational, financial, legal, and political concerns. An important aspect is that the leaders of such an organization are no longer the peers of the researchers but, rather, persons who are often not well-versed in the material. The emphasis comes to lie on the formal aspects of projects and far less on the content. Possibly even more difficult are interdisciplinary projects in which, par excellence, what is important is that at least a few participants are well-versed in all the domains in question. Hyperspecialization – sustained as well by the vertical structure – hinders interdisciplinarity, nonetheless an essential factor for attaining progressive insight as well as innovation. With some *bons mots* as caveats: "Research consists of knowing more and more about less and less, until you ultimately know everything about nothing." Let us, on the contrary, open the windows wide, let the air flow inside, and continue to think about investigation in an open, interdisciplinary way. It is vital for art and science alike.

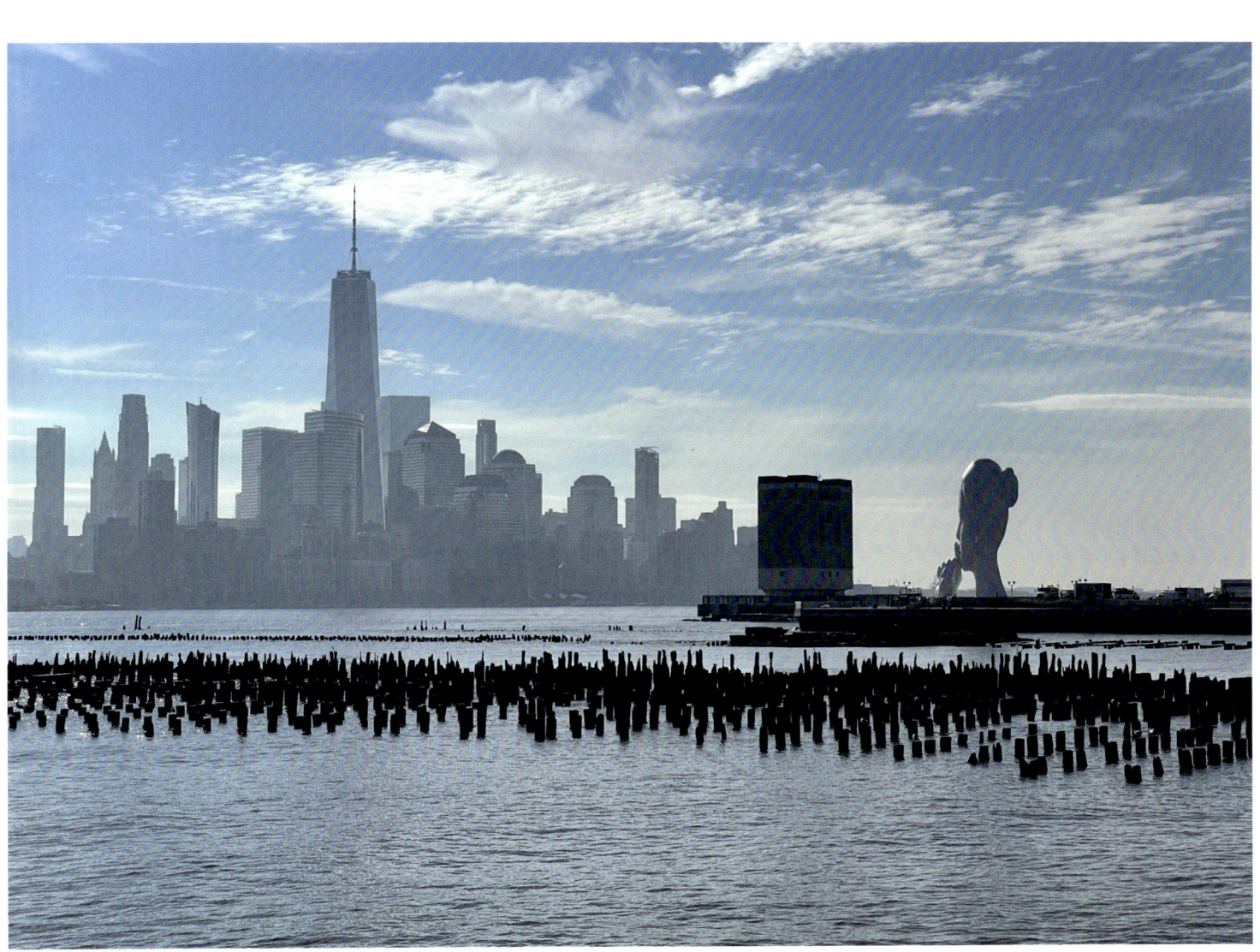

For a large part, Vesalius's trailblazing work lives on in our spirit thanks to the outstanding illustrations in his *De Humani Corporis Fabrica*. They were drawn by the hand of the German-born Italian Jan van Kalkar, who had learned the subject from Titian. The poses and the settings for the dissected human bodies were expressly artistic and allegorical, but Kalkar's art also comprised much new optical knowledge in particular. The magic of the *Fabrica* lies in this interplay of science and art. That is why it is so terribly appropriate that Jaume Plensa's *Four Elements* acquires a place at the Leuven University Library and on the Hertogen site, near the future Vesalius Museum.

Notes

1   Alva Noë, *Strange Tools: Art and Human Nature* (New York: Farrar, Straus and Giroux; Hill and Wang, 2015).
2   Martin Heidegger, *Being and Time* (Albany, NY: SUNY Press, 1996).
3   Hanna Arendt, *The Human Condition* (Chicago: Univ. of Chicago Press, 1958).
4   Martin Schulze, "Jaume Plensa's stunning larger-than-life sculptures (Jan. 23, 2017)," https://publicdelivery.org/jaume-plensa-sculptures/.
5   Gerpho 3D, "'2D½' sculpture: *Sanna* by Jaume Plensa [2016 2023]," https://sketchfab.com/3d-models/2d12-sculpture-sanna-by-jaume-plensa-b4c354c2b7b3407297f7117638c2f2b0.
6   M.A. González Virgen, *Artistic Research in the Visual Arts: Definitions and the Quest for Paradigms*, PhD thesis KU Leuven, 2017.
7   Katrin Busch and Dieter Lesage, eds., *A portrait of the artist as a researcher. The Academy and the Bologna Process* (Antwerp: Museum van Hedendaagse Kunst, 2007); and Tom Holert, "Art in the Knowledge-based Polis," *e-flux Journal* 3 (2009), https://www.e-flux.com/journal/03/68537/art-in-the-knowledge-based-polis/.
8   Dieter Lesage, "Tegen het supplement - Enkele beschouwingen over artistiek onderzoek," *FORUM+* 24, no. 1 (2017): 4-11, https://doi.org/10.5117/FORUM2017.1.LESA.
9   Jeroen Brouwers, *Sunken Red*, trans. A. Dixon (New York: New Amsterdam, 1988).
10 Erik Thys,"De potloodmethode," *DW B* 2021, no. 3 (september): 7-12.

11 Martin Heidegger, "The Age of the World Picture" (1938), in *The Question Concerning Technology and Other Essays*, ed. and transl. W. Lovitt (New York: Harper Torchbooks, 1977), 115-154, here p. 125. See also: Germán Toro-Pérez, "On the difference between artistic research and artistic practice," in *Art and artistic research*, ed. C. Caduff, F. Siegenthaler, and T. Wälchli (Zurich: Verlag Scheidegger & Spiess AG, 2010), 30-39.

Literature cited

Arendt, Hanna. *The Human Condition*. Chicago: Univ. of Chicago Press, 1958.

Brouwers, Jeroen. *Sunken Red*. Translated by A. Dixon. New York: New Amsterdam, 1988.

Busch, Katrin, and Dieter Lesage, eds. *A portrait of the artist as a researcher. The Academy and the Bologna Process*. Antwerp: Museum van Hedendaagse Kunst, 2007.

Gerpho 3D. "'2D'½ sculpture: *Sanna* by Jaume Plensa [2016 2023]." https://sketchfab.com/3d-models/2d12-sculpture-sanna-by-jaume-plensa-b4c-354c2b7b3407297f7117638c2f2b0. Accessed 2024-3-30.

González Virgen, M.A. *Artistic Research in the Visual Arts: Definitions and the Quest for Paradigms*, (*Artistiek onderzoek in de visuele kunsten: Definities en de zoektocht naar paradigma's*), 2017. PhD Thesis, KU Leuven.

Heidegger, Martin. Being and Time. Translated by Joan Stambaugh. Albany, NY: SUNY Press, 1996.

Heidegger, Martin. "The Age of the World Picture" (1938). In *The Question Concerning Technology and Other Essays*, edited and translated by W. Lovitt, 115-154. New York: Harper Torchbooks, 1977.

Tom Holert, "Art in the Knowledge-based Polis." *e-flux Journal* 3 (2009). https://www.e-flux.com/journal/03/68537/art-in-the-knowledge-based-polis/.

Lesage, Dieter. "Tegen het supplement – Enkele beschouwingen over artistiek onderzoek." *FORUM+* 24, no. 1 (2017): 4-11. https://doi.org/10.5117/FORUM2017.1.LESA.

Noë, Alva. *Strange Tools: Art and Human Nature*. New York: Farrar, Straus and Giroux; Hill and Wang, 2015

Schulze, Martin. "Jaume Plensa's Stunning Larger-than-life Sculptures [Jan. 23, 2017]." https://publicdelivery.org/jaume-plensa-sculptures/. Accessed 2024-3-30.

Toro-Pérez, Germán. "On the difference between artistic research and artistic practice." In *Art and artistic research*, edited by C. Caduff, F. Siegenthaler, and T. Wälchli, 30-39. Zurich: Verlag Scheidegger & Spiess AG, 2010.

Thys, Erik. "De potloodmethode." *DW B* 2021, no. 3 (September): 7-12.

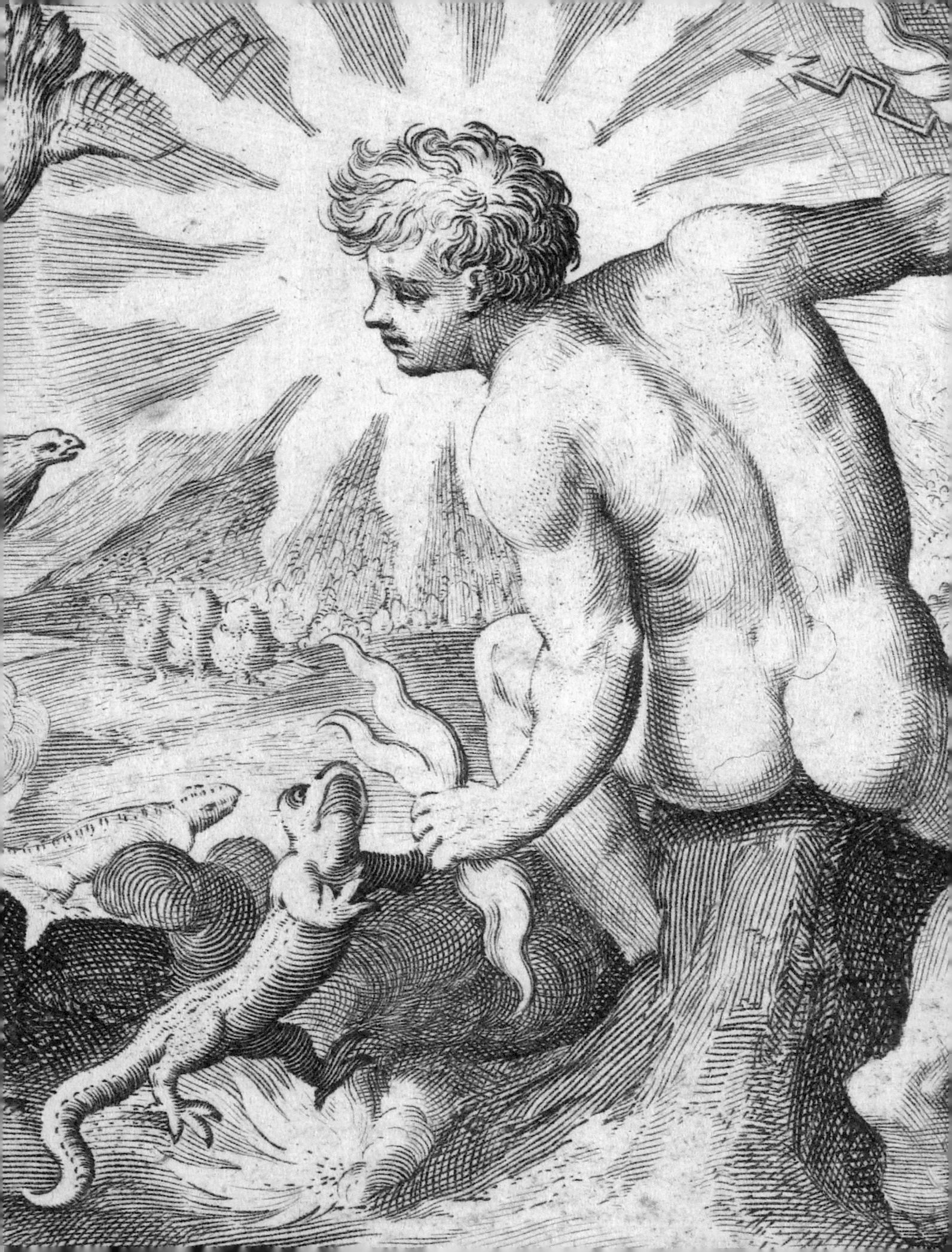

The Four Elements

Mark Derez

Jaume Plensa has baptized his work *The Four Elements*. He stationed *Fire* at the University Library, while the other three elements have been here on the Hertogen site put into a kind of pillar of salt, in which their faces have turned to stone. This particular pillar of salt has to a certain degree remained dynamic: it is a twisted pillar, like a helix in genetics, which is not out of place in a medical context. You could venture to say it is a totem pole or, similarly, a tabernacle with figures that radiate calm, serenity, and interiority.

With *The Four Elements*, Plensa has tapped into a very old cask, a body of thought that goes back to antiquity, to the so-called Axial Age (Jaspers's *Achsenzeit*) between 800 and 200 B.C., the time when religion and philosophy were making their breakthrough. What follows is a very summary historical excursus, making a long story short. The so-called pre-Socratics, or Ionian natural philosophers, had been racking their brains over the problem of unity and plurality and changeability. Confronted with the plurality of things – which, moreover, were subject to change – they went in search of the *archè*, the very first principle. Yet they kept their feet on the ground and, being down-to-earth, sought for a basic material out of which they supposed the entire world had been constructed. Thales of Miletus (600 B.C.) thought of water; Parmenides (500 B.C.) considered both fire and water; and Heraclitus (500 B.C.) put forward three basic components: earth, air, and water, which were merely manifestations of fire, the original element. Then the crowning achievement came along: Empedocles (who died in 430 B.C.) became the first to formulate the doctrine of the Four Elements.

Detail from Nicolaas de Bruyn,
Ignis, part of the emblem series
The Four Elements, first half 17th
century. Engraving.

Aristotle (384–321 B.C.) was not quite completely content with this *quadriga* and imported a fifth chief material, the *quinta essentia*: aether, with which the sphere of the heavenly bodies was supposedly permeated. All the same, in the terrestrial sphere the chief role was assigned to the Four Elements. Even more important, according to Aristotle, was that the earthly elements were not primordial. More decisive instead proved to be the fundamental properties of matter: cold, hot, wet, dry. From the combination of those qualities, all of reality could be explained. Earth was cold and dry, Water cold and wet, Air hot and wet, and Fire hot and dry. In a subsequent time, the seasons, too, would be associated by analogy: winter with Water, spring with Air, summer with Fire, and fall with Earth.

Elements and temperaments

Hippocrates (*c.* 460-*c.* 370 B.C.) and Galen (125–199 A.D.) introduced the doctrine of the Four Elements into medicine. Elements were related to bodily fluids and temperaments. The low-spirited melancholic is identified with Earth; the hydropic phlegmatic with Water; the sanguine, who has blood in excess, with Air; and the choleric, with the short fuse, with the element Fire. The entire body of thought relies on analogies, with metaphors as its vehicle. Later on, moral properties would thus be ascribed to the Four Elements as well, though not necessarily as positive qualifications. Air, for example, was equated with affectation – the traditional *vanitas* motif, vanity of vanities. The identification is obvious, seeing as in the Hebrew scriptures there is indeed mention of 'Air and Emptiness' (translating literally here from the new Dutch version of Ecclesiastes 1): "Air, vanity of vanities, it is all emptiness."

The Stoics (from 300 B.C. onward) had been satisfied with these Four Elements, taking fire to be the dynamic *archè*. Much later, Arab alchemists added mercury and sulfur. In the sixteenth century, Paracelsus focused on three elements: mercury, sulfur, and salt. Alchemy always remained on the outside track. In the long run, Aristotle came out the genuine winner, and he would leave his stamp on the academic curriculum at all universities, enduringly defining instruction in logic and the natural sciences (*physica*), in particular. In the twelfth and thirteenth centuries, Aristotle was rediscovered at the newly founded universities. Thomas Aquinas poured Aristotle into the mold of scholasticism, which was considerably broad-minded. Only ancient concepts that flagrantly contradicted Christian teaching were banned, which was not the case with the Four Elements. These were sacrosanct well into the eighteenth century. They are reasonably present in the lecture notes at Leuven. At times they show up there in delightful illustrations, as students had the habit of prettying up their notes with pictures and drawings.

In his *Physica* lecture notes, under the chapter titled "De Aqua" (On Water), Hendrik van Cantelbeke – a student in 1669–1670 at The Lily, one of the four pedagogies of the Leuven Faculty of Arts – includes two prints: an etching by the French engraver Jacques Callot (1592–1635), who was quite popular with the students; and, in addition, an engraving from the Northern Netherlands with, shall we say, a moralizing bent. A physician, medicaster, or quack holds up a urinal to assess the sick person's liquid through the transmitted light. In this case, the urine comes from the chambermaid: "ons kamenier, het soete dier, zij heeft geweest bij Klaas of Pier" (roughly: our lady's maid, who's so very sweet, has probably been with Claus or Pete). It was, then, a pregnancy test, as well as an edifying tableau from the 'Holland School' for decorating Hendrik's dictation (as notes were called at that time).

The elements in prints

Over time, especially in the sixteenth and seventeenth centuries, the Four Elements have occasioned an enormous production in images, including complete artistic cycles, series of paintings, and sets of prints. The center of it all was in the Low Countries, with big names like Jan Bruegel the Elder and Abraham Janssens as well as, in the graphic arts, Antonie Wierix II and Hendrik Goltzius. Sometimes, to boot, the elements are implicitly present in landscapes with the four seasons. Or they are disguised as genre paintings, including the unquestionable apex: the market and kitchen pieces by Joachim Beuckelaer (1534–1574) which are known as *The Four Elements*, but which unfortunately moved from the Museum of Fine Arts (MSK) in Ghent to the National Gallery in London in 2001.

For representing the elements, artists were able to draw from a rich reservoir. In his *Iconologia* from 1593, Cesare Ripa offered one manual for doing so, which was, according to the subtitle, a description of universal depictions from antiquity and other places. In the Dutch translation from 1644, they are called *Uytbeeldingen des Verstands* (roughly: The Mind's Representations).

Ripa provides personifications as well as an entire arsenal of attributes. The descriptions in and of themselves are quite visual and picturesque.

Earth is the lowest, heaviest, yet smallest element, and the undermost part of the gigantic cosmos. Earth is represented as an elderly woman with a gray dress that turtles crawl across, as well as with a green cloak of herbs, flowers, grapes, and ears of grain. A horn of plenty has to be included. On her head she bears a city and on her shoulders two pyramids. And she is suckling a child ('de borsten zal ze buiten bloot vertonen' [her breasts she will display bare, in the open]). Water is a naked woman in the midst of sea monsters. She leans on a water jug, and her head is decorated with a garland of reeds, her neck with a collar of coral. For her brassiere: two large shells 'die de gestalte van de borsten vertonen' (that portray the shape of her breasts). The artist does not need to leave much to the imagination. Underneath a rainbow, another lady appears in a translucent garment with wavy hair. She is Air. She is accompanied by a peacock, dedicated to Juno, and by a chameleon, an animal that does not eat or drink, but lives only from the wind and is nourished by air, as Pliny relates. Fire occupies the highest place: a woman surrounded by salamanders, with a phoenix immolating itself on her head, and with Jupiter's lightning bolt in her right hand. She is accompanied by Vulcan, who handles the hot coals, and by Vesta, who keeps the fire burning.

Nicolaas de Bruyn (redux)

Visual artists swim in a stream of associations. They do not necessarily have to adhere to Ripa's book of recipes. They like to color outside the lines too much for that. Let us take, for example, the Antwerp engraver Nicolaas de Bruyn (1571–1656), a namesake of the Leuven sculptor, though he lived two centuries later. This Nicolaas de Bruyn (redux) did not sculpt any images but scratched them out in copper. For his copper engravings he took inspiration from the work of Maarten de Vos (1531–1603), a contemporary of Pieter Bruegel the Elder. De Bruyn's four-part cycle about the Elements dates from around 1600.

It revolves around typical emblemata, symbolic images with a title or a motto and an explanatory caption. For his inventions De Bruyn (and/or De Vos) proved to adhere reasonably well to Ripa's *Iconologia*. The boxes for a

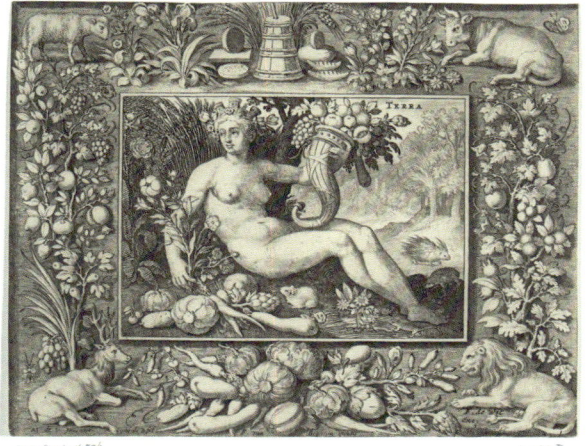
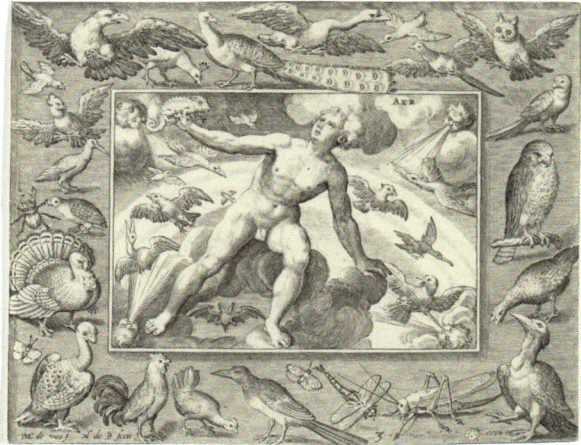
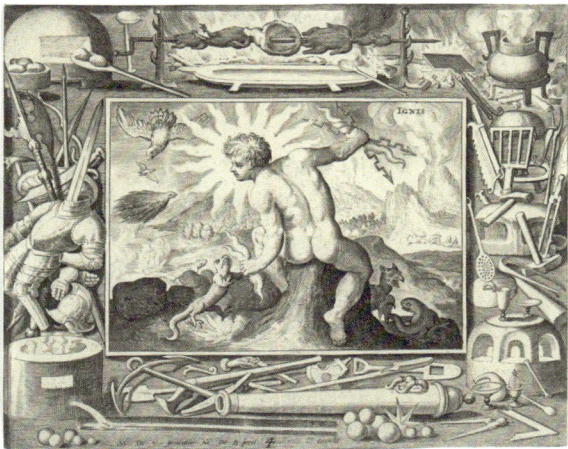
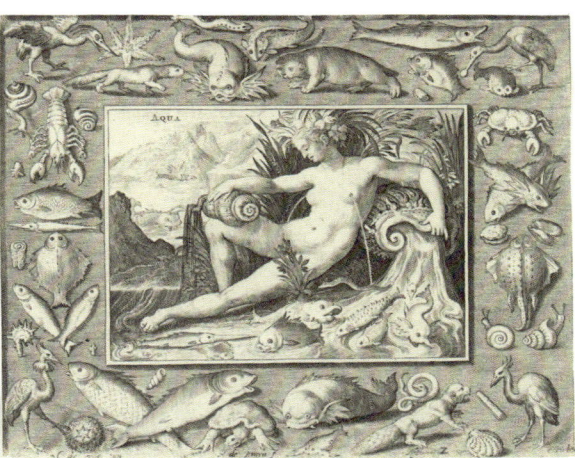

Nicolaas de Bruyn, left to right: *Terra, Aer, Ignis* and *Aqua*, part of the emblem series The Four Elements, first half 17th century. Engraving.

horn of plenty, water jug, a chameleon, Juno's peacock, and Jupiter's lightning all get checked. Though we encountered no dragons in Ripa's case, they turn up here as concerns Fire. In terms of gender, the artist shows himself to be flexible: Air and Fire have become men with eye-catching musculature.

Barnyard and wild animals alike are in the pasture around Earth; the additional features for Water are teeming with fishes (and mussels!); and for Air there is a yard full of fowl with, among other things, a turkey: poultry from the New World. The additional features for Fire offer an oven catalog: a smelting furnace, a potter's kiln, and a baker's oven. Furthermore, there are ironmonger's wares, blacksmith's equipment, and war armaments on offer, as well as a panoply of spears and armor on sale. The center of the image flashingly flaunts a roasting spit. As the caption states, Fire is indispensable for a savory cuisine; it lends flavor to the dishes. The Latin inscriptions definitely do not eschew small talk and domestic, house-and-garden philosophizing. There is a certain sensuality that speaks from them, one traditionally connected to the Southern Netherlands. The excessively ornate frames for the prints are no doubt invaluably indebted to the margin illuminations in the so-called Flemish art of the miniature.

A late representative in the genre was the outsized canvas that a Leuven burgomaster gave to his town in 1744, an allegory of the Four Elements by a local artist, B. Beschey (1708–1776). The elements are personified as figures from the Roman world of the gods, along with their attributes: Earth as Ceres with a sheaf of wheat, Air as Juno with her peacock, Fire as Vulcan with his blacksmith's hammer, and for Water a river god who has remained anonymous (the Dyle River?) with a water jug. Even the color composition is characterized by the elements: brown (earth), blue (air), green (water), and red (fire).

Making a comeback

In Louis XV's France, the elements were still being put on stage. In the *Ballet des Elémens*, the very young king himself danced, too. More well known is *Les Elémens*, the 'dance symphony' by Jean Féry Rebel from 1737. The elements were represented in orchestration that was amazingly new. Rebel had in mind a kind of absolute music, the music of the spheres (the way Pythagoras himself supposedly heard it). Yet despite how forward-looking (at times even atonal) Rebel's music was, it became the swan song for the genre and for the Four Elements in general.

In the second half of the eighteenth century, the gods tumbled from the heavens, and demystification spread at a furious speed. The Enlightenment became the delivery room for new elements, detected at a deeper level by way of analysis. Hydrogen was discovered in 1766, oxygen in 1772, carbon in 1775, and sulfur in 1777. At the end of the process in 1789, Antoine Lavoisier published a list of 33 kinds of chemical matter that could not be broken down any further. In Dmitri Mendeleev's Periodic Table of the Elements, so-called, the number at present runs to 119.

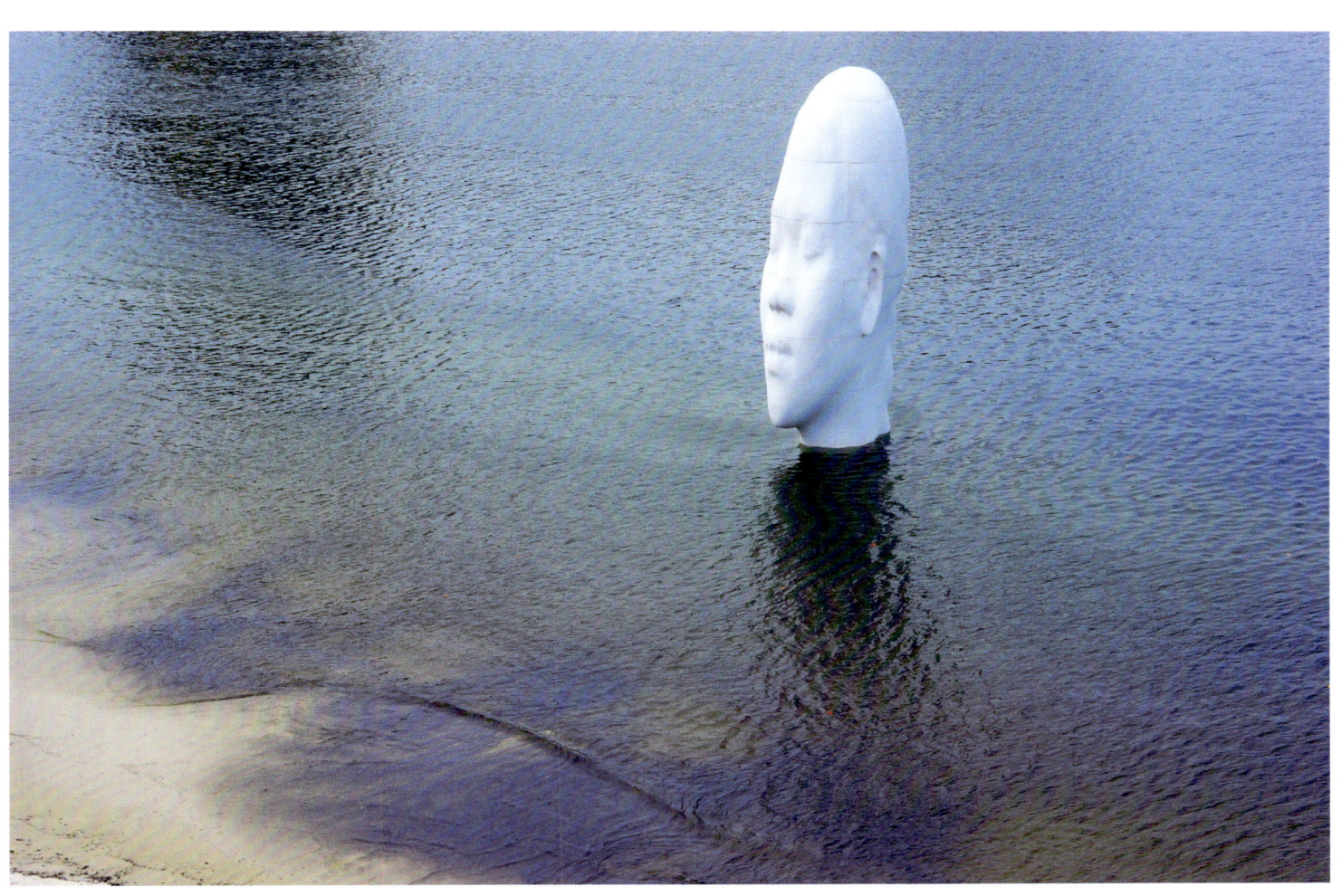

In Leuven, the laboratory for experimental physics was inaugurated in 1766, for which the court architect Laurent-Benoît Dewez had reconstructed the old premises of the Faculty of Arts, adding a neoclassical portico, at that time an absolute novelty: avant-garde architecture for innovative scientific research. In this inventive climate, the last Aristotelian treatises on physics were cleared from the table, and the Four Elements ended up in the waste basket. Just like miracle stories and Marian apparitions, the doctrine of the Four Elements was unable to handle the increasingly mechanized worldview.

One hundred years later, in the second half of the nineteenth century, botanists left the systematically ordered beds in the botanical gardens to immerse themselves in cell biology behind microscopes in their labs. As a result of continually progressing specialization, alienation also entered the stage, and the overview was lost for the wider public. Cultural historians discern a timid return of the Four Elements in the ecological movement, where the quality of the soil (earth), air, and water, as well as the sustainability of energy (fire) are high on the agenda. In the natural sciences, an interdisciplinary approach with emphatic attention toward ecosystems has gained the right to exist. Connectedness is crucial. A new understanding of the Four Elements seems to be able to preserve the Blue Planet from downfall, after all.

Literature cited

Berger, Susanna. *The Art of Philosophy: Visual Thinking in Europe from the Late Renaissance to the Early Enlightenment*. Princeton, NJ: Princeton Univ. Press, 2017.

Böhme, Gernot, and Hartmut Böhme. *Feuer, Wasser, Erde, Luft. Eine Kulturgeschichte der Elemente*. Munich: C.H. Beck, 2014.

Lehner-Jobst, Claudia, and Veronika Sandbichler, eds. *One World – Macht der 4 Elemente*. Vienna: König, 2022. Exhibition catalog.

Vandenghoer, Carl, ed. *300 Jaar Chemie te Leuven, 1685–1985*. Leuven: Ceuterick, 1985.

Vanpaemel, Geert, Katharina Smeyers, An Smets, and Diewer van der Meijden, eds. Ex Cathedra: *De Leuvense collegedictaten van de 16de tot de 18de eeuw*. Leuven: Universiteitsbibliotheek KU Leuven, 2012.

Veenbaas, Jabik. *De Verlichting als kraamkamer. Over het tijdperk en zijn betekenis voor het heden*, Amsterdam: Nieuw Amsterdam, 2013.

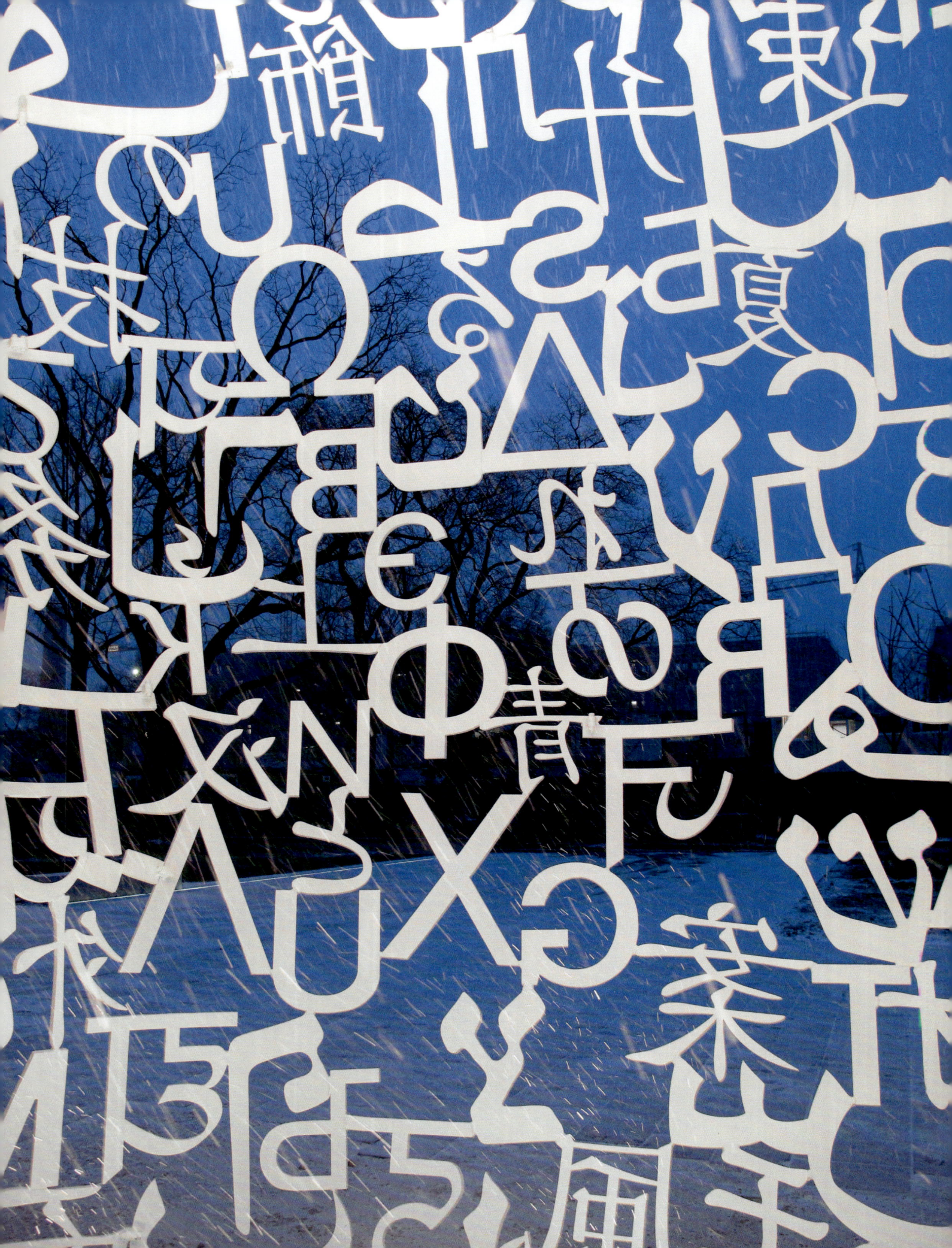

A Skin of Language

Tom Van Imschoot

A sculpture is not an object, it is an interrogation, a question, a response.
—Alberto Giacometti[1]

Some sculptures of Jaume Plensa have a skin of language. Their contours consist of a lattice of letters, welded to one another from various alphabets, which give shape to human figures, sitting steadfastly in a contemplative stance. It makes an image of how language is the elemental material that forms our bodily existence, delimiting yet opening it up for others. What is intriguing, though, is that Plensa's language figures incarnate at the same time a sculpted stillness, a stillness that seems to be their core while also encircling them. How does this tension between language, stillness, body, and sculpture relate to a multilingual world in accelerated times?

For ages, the language of sculpture has been prominently associated with an experience of stillness, silence – in short, the absence of any verbal language. This does not result from sculptures literally not speaking, for paintings do not do so, either. It results from the art of sculpting 'speaking' via the materiality of bodies and forms at a standstill, with space as the connecting medium.

Sculpture distinguishes itself from the other arts, as the sculptor Philip Van Isacker writes in his book *De sculptura* (2017), because it does not depict reality, but rather makes it itself. "Not the illusion of what is real, but what is real itself is produced [...]."[2] Eye-to-eye with a sculpture, according to Van Isacker, we stand opposite a resuming and compressed way of reflecting about reality which has itself become a material reality in real space.

Consequently, the art of sculpting is inevitably related to the human body, whether it represents it figuratively or not. No matter the time, place, or culture it comes from, as a result of its spatial materiality a sculpture shares the here and now of its viewers, after all, there where their own bodies are situated. That is why the human body remains the "first and most self-evident subject" of sculpture as well, says Van Isacker, even in its abstract or conceptual forms. "As long as the body is the seat of human thinking and feeling," he writes, "the art of sculpting, as a medium that attempts to delve into what is elementally human, will always use the body anew as its subject."[3] For Van Isacker, sculpture responds to "the need experienced time and again to compress thinking and feeling into an image."[4] In the process, the body is indispensable because it "alone is not only the carrier of the rational aspect, but also bears the totality of what is human, and because it admits of as many different representations as the complexity presented by the existence of humankind itself."[5]

Sculpture, therefore, speaks not only to but also with the language of the body. And that language is primarily non-verbal, not bound to the *logos* (or the *ratio* that human beings derive from it), but gestural and affective. It is what sculpture has in common with dance, with the difference being that the movement of the body via the deliberate medium of sculpture is utterly reduced to stillness. It is the spectator who moves and may be moved by the tension between standstill and movement which is materialized in a sculpture, not as an immutable theme, but as a specific compression of cultural tensions.

Anyone, for example, who ends up standing in front of *Mother with her Dead Son* (1937–1939) by Käthe Kollwitz at the Neue Wache (New Guardhouse) in Berlin, does not need to know anything about the sculptor's biography or even the history of Germany to be able to read the stilled body language of the sculpture. Substantive digressions and underlying narratives fall by the wayside to make room for a statue that makes a moment stand still, just as any monument is in essence meant to do, and which recalls, here and now, how a time converted the personal pain of the violence of war into reflection.

Who does not read into the serene body language of this twentieth-century pietà how the continued love of a mother overrides the defeated character of a fallen child/soldier? Who does not fall silent by how this quadruply enlarged version of Kollwitz's original is dwarfed by the monumental nineteenth-century space, which has been dedicated to the "victims of war and tyranny" since 1993? And who, in the middle of that resounding contrast, does not hear, precisely as a result of the incongruity, how the sculpture shapes a lasting material echo of the unseen and anonymous suffering caused by war? It is a lament for a body that has returned dead to the body that gave it life, just for a moment still tenderly embraced by sorrow, borne with dignity yet on the verge of the unbearable.

Words are not needed. We are reading actual body language, placed in a real space, and it is their tension that resounds in our own silenced body. Here, indeed, does an image of what is elementally human appear, as an expression of resistance against a time that squandered human life *en masse*, with the very means that sculpture has at hand as a medium. It tells the specific fate of a woman, a mother, a sculptor from a time past, but even those who do not know that see how the statue is generally laid bare to the elements, by way of the open oculus it is placed under. The serene resistance of this image remains vulnerable, it seems to say, unguarded in the Neue Wache. And in watching it, one starts to wonder: where indeed does the elementally human finds shelter? The body, though, is still; it is the material that speaks.

Language as visual material

It may well require a detour by way of poetry – this art that employs language, in fact, as material – in order to see how the material language of sculpture nonetheless touches on the language of the word. In his renowned ekfrasis "Archaic Torso of Apollo" (1908) – a poem, like Keats's "Ode on a Graecian Urn," inspired by the visual arts – Rainer Maria Rilke evokes how the gleaming image of a Greek male torso (without a head, genitals, or limbs) appeals to him like an oracle, with the imperative closing line: "Du mußt dein Leben ändern." ("You must change your life.")

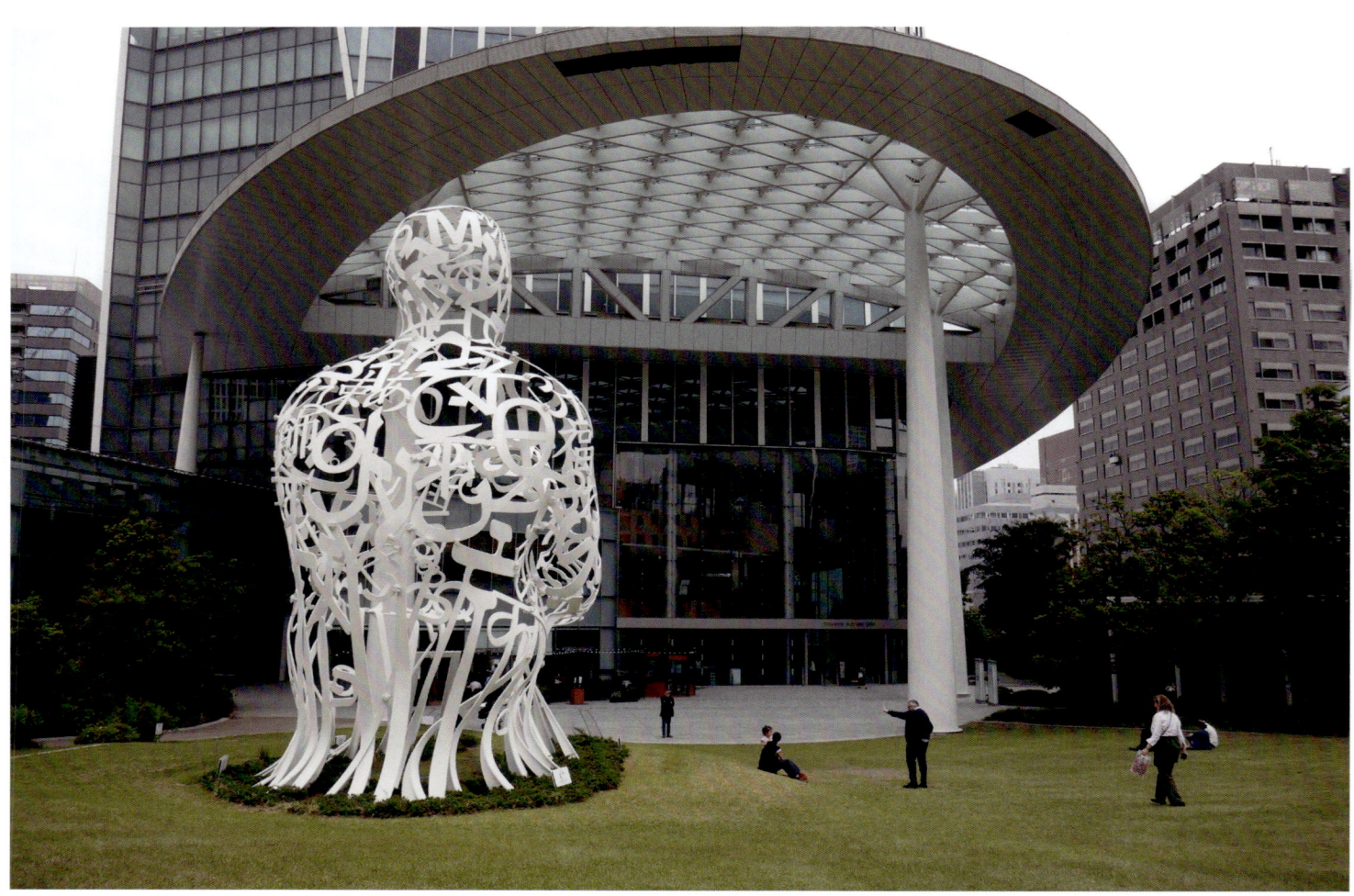

The voice seems to come from nowhere. It is as if the poet is masquerading, with the archaic torso as a ventriloquist doll, that he is in fact speaking to himself when admonishing change, in a mixture of projection and imaginary identification. Upon closer inspection, however, Rilke calls forth an echo of the sculpture itself with this voice, in his own language. Word after word, image after image, comparison after comparison, he lyrically composes how the deformed chunk of what was once a classical sculpture suspends all its deficiencies in the form that survives. The missing head appears in the physical body, and a smiling gaze bounces back the gaze of the viewer, with the blinding glow of a star that breaks out of its borders. The observing poet thus suddenly becomes the observed, as if he himself is turned to stone. And the voice that calls him evokes therefore nothing other than the vital capacity for change, which speaks for him from the sculpture itself.[6]

It is, then, sculpture's art of metamorphosis, its mute capacity for going beyond its material limitations and for keeping any standstill in motion, that Rilke's visual language resonates. That reverberation is no coincidence when you consider that in those years he had given his poetry a new wrinkle, more oriented toward things, in close proximity to the art of sculpture as the secretary to Auguste Rodin. Crucial, however, is that in this poem he allows his language to be infiltrated literally as well by the voice of sculpture, as a commandment that reveals to him how he needs to go on. With verbal and visual rhyme Rilke probes the Greek sculpture, allowing its material language to be absorbed into that of his poetry, so as to have it appear as a model for how to change one's self and to break out of a petrified standstill. In this way, Rilke makes of his language something material itself in the end, a bodily material, a skin – continually on the edge of petrification, yet also capable of feeling, of being moved and, within that movement, renewing and revolutionizing itself. In tune with the language of the sculpture's material, Rilke's poetry allows the materiality of language itself to break out.

Over a half century later, a young poet goes further down the same trail, in a way that changes his life even more radically. In 1964, the 40-year-old Marcel Broodthaers seals up a few unsold copies of his fourth collection of poems *Pense-bête* (Reminder, 1963) in plaster, so that they cannot be read anymore, thus realizing his first visual work, a sculpture indeed. Surrealism meets conceptualism. The young poet had wondered whether he would then also not be able to sell anything "et réussir dans la vie" (and succeed in life), as he wrote in the invitation for the exhibition preview. And he added, in a bitingly sober way: "L'idée enfin d'inventer quelque chose d'insincère me traversa l'esprit en je me mis aussitôt au travail" (Finally, the idea of inventing something insincere crossed my mind, and I immediately got to work [on it]). The word play à la Magritte – which unveils the thinking animal in the collection's title already as 'silly' ("la pense-bête" is also a dumb idea, a *pensée bête*) – thus acquires a gestural allure à la Duchamp. It pillories the stupidity of the commercial art world by using its insincerity against it. Romanticism becomes pragmaticism; an unsold collection of poetry becomes a successful work of visual art.

In the same move, Broodthaers's poetic language acquires a material skin. On the one hand, it renders his poetry definitively unreadable; on the other hand, it also protects it like a suit of armor. Broodthaers places it, in fact, as a hermetic object on a pedestal, sovereignly rejecting the desire for readability and accessibility. Yet in doing so the sculpture allows Broodthaers, ironically enough, to emphasize also the materiality of language – its everyday abstraction.

It forms the beginning of an artistic oeuvre in which the discursive conventions of the visual arts (its signatures, its figures, its taxonomies, the order of the modern museum itself...) as well as the graphic infrastructure of literature are constantly held up to each other's light. With the mussel as a template (*La grande casserole de moules*, 1966), he exploits the plastic potential of language, in a conceptual game with symbol and sculpture, at the same time democratic and hermetically closed. And he continually inverts readable and unreadable, drawing on the ambiguous tension between the visual arts and literature. In 1969, for instance, he accentuates the rhythmic visuality of Mallarmé's collection of typographical poetry *Un coup de dés jamais n'abolira le hasard* (1897, translated as *A Roll of the Dice Will Never Abolish Chance* by Robert Bononno and Jeff Clark, 2015), by printing an exact copy in which every word is covered with a small bar of black ink. And that same year, in the film *La pluie (projet pour un texte)* (Rain [Project for a Text]), he stages how ink drains away from the pen of a overtly romantic writer (whom he himself 'plays'), as a result of an excess of water that gushes downward like 'rain' from a barely hidden watering can above his head. Signification is both blocked and becoming elusive. Verbal language turns into visual material.

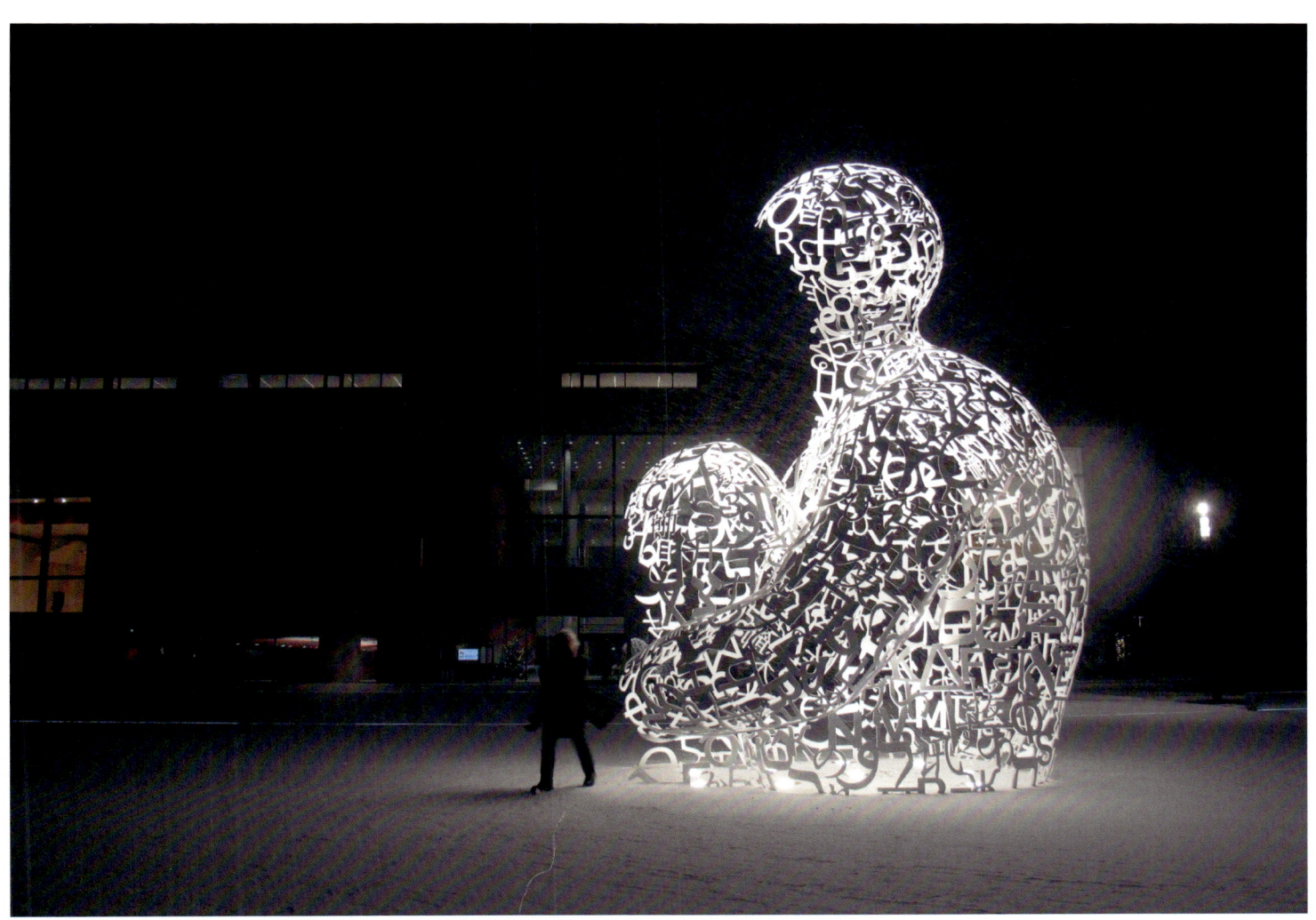

Words like clay

In this way, language also becomes freely useable material when the art of sculpture expands its traditional arsenal with entirely new techniques, materials, and installations in the '60s and '70s, in response to how conceptual art questions its foundations. With his iconic *One and Three Chairs* (1965), the neon *Four Colors Four Words (Orange-Violet-Green-Blue)* (1966), or the self-aware metawork *Titled (Art as Idea as Idea) The Word 'Definition'* (1966–1968), *Art & Language* member Joseph Kosuth provided textbook examples for what that conceptual questioning looks like. Yet, with a drawing such as *A heap of Language* (1966), however, Land Artist Robert Smithson showed how artists could use verbal language as concrete material, too. Via a pyramidal piling-up of words that themselves name all sorts of language forms ("speech," "vernacular," "tongue"...), he built a sculpture on paper. One could see it as a verbal equivalent of his large-scale earthworks, and it really reads as a 'mission statement': any artwork speaks about the material of which it itself consists.

A similar attention for language as physical material surfaces in the concentrated 'statements' by Lawrence Weiner, who grounded his sculpting practice in conceptual art at the end of the '60s, and who has since almost exclusively limited himself to the use of words as raw material. In museums, in books, on manhole covers, and on walls in public spaces, he puts compact phrases like *Earth to Earth Ashes to Ashes Dust to Dust* (1970) or *A Bit of Matter And A Little Bit More* (1976). They are statements that derive their verbal components from the basic resource of ordinary language, they use words like clay, democratically accessible and available to everyone. Placing them in space, they acquire sculptural weight. The art of sculpture to which Weiner has always considered himself as belonging, no longer depicts any body; it addresses the body of the viewer itself. In passing by, the viewer is momentarily invited to relate to the programmatically open relationship put into view by rudimentary phrases like *To See and Be Seen* (1972) or *Bits and Pieces Put Together To Present a Semblance of A Whole* (2005).

This is the very principle of minimalist art at work, where representation is traced back to a minimum in order to create, in fact, maximum attention to the dialogue between an object and space, including the viewer. To be sure, restriction to words, as in Weiner's case, was seldom on the agenda for most minimalist artists; but they paved the way for sculptors like him by an utter

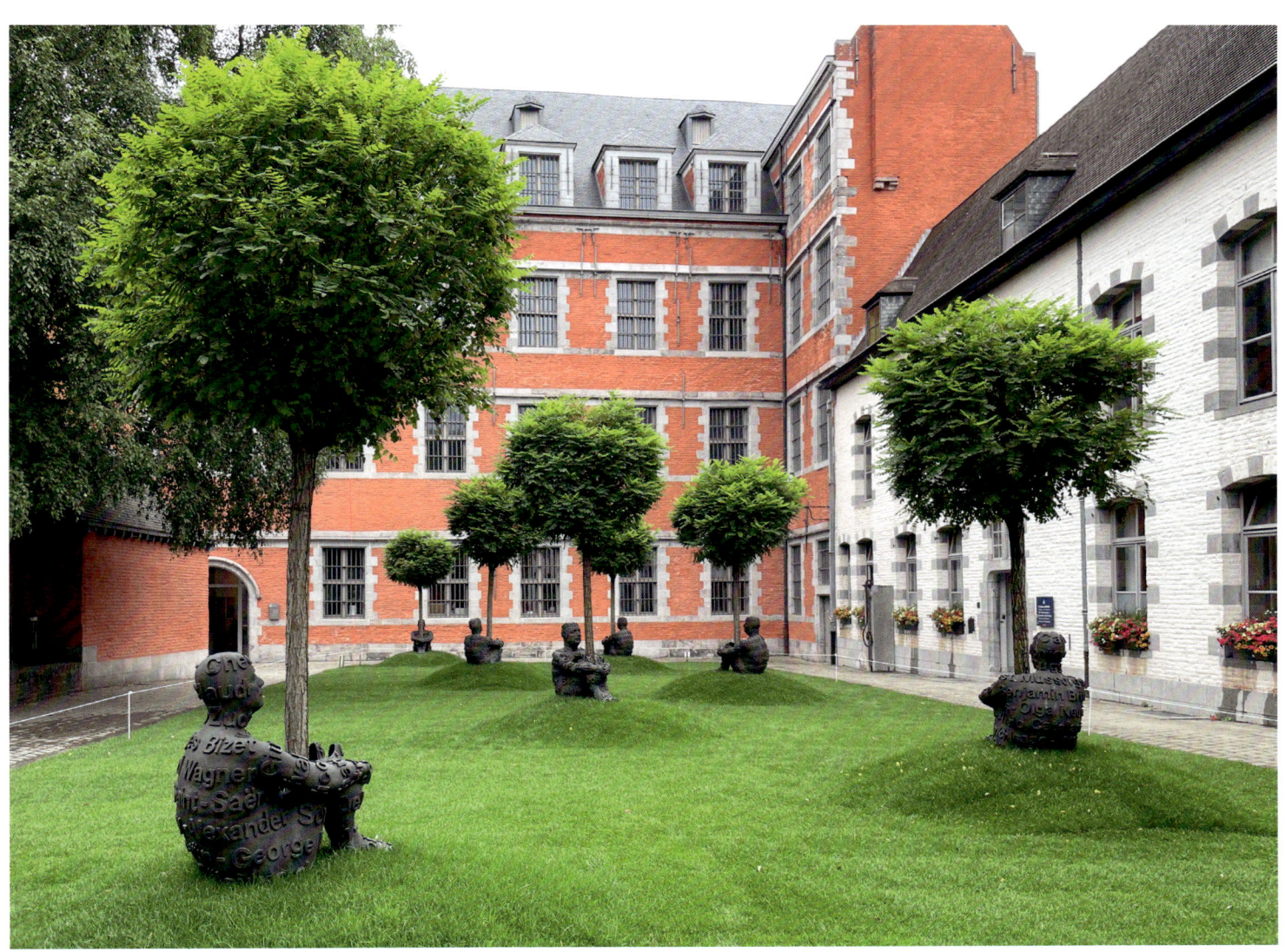

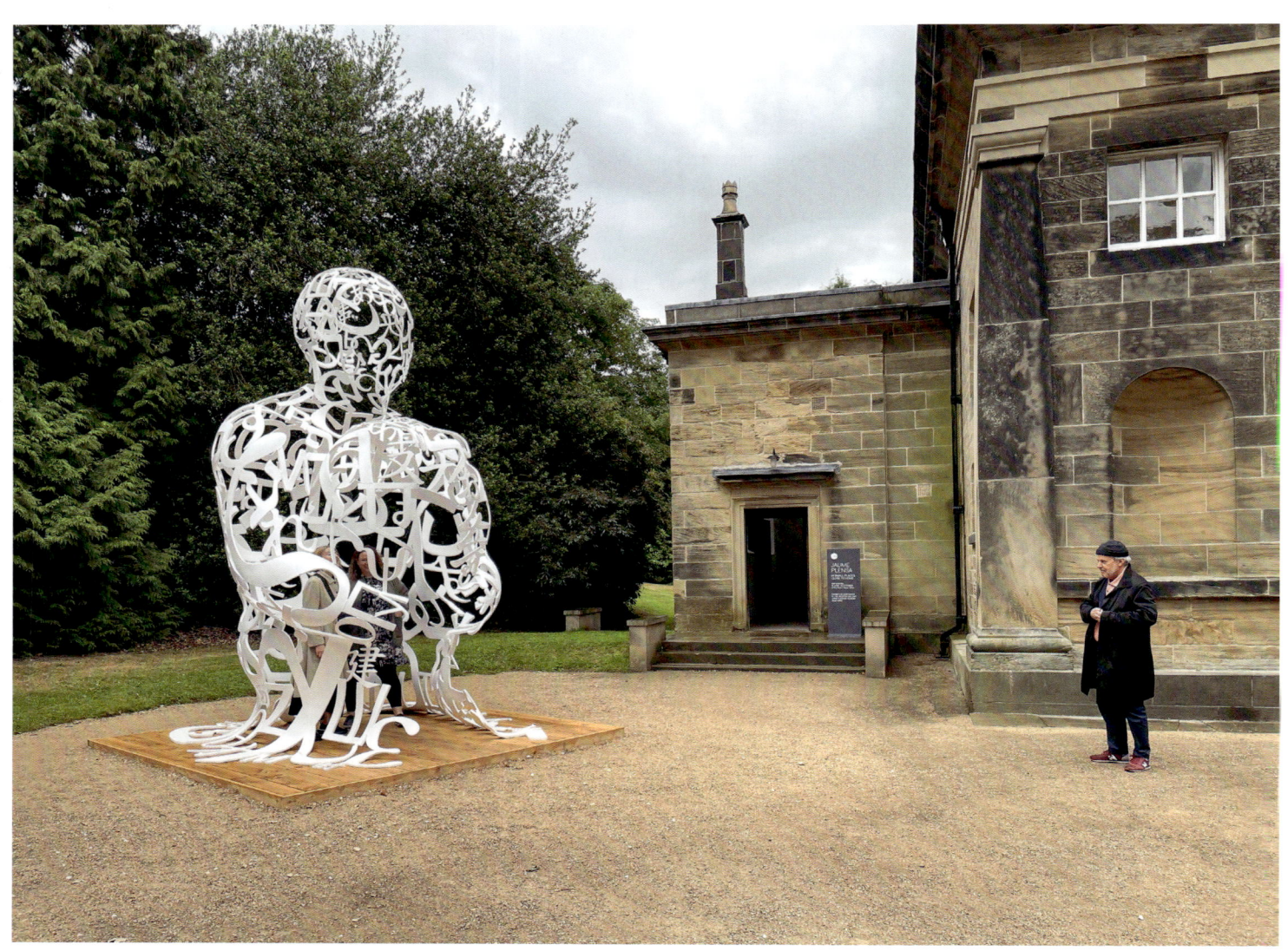

reduction of sculptures to their naked materiality and the bodily tension that arises from it. Carl André for instance – who constructed poems, too, with language as a material object – built material obstructions that read like mental instructions for bodily movement. In the case of Bernd Lohaus's sculptures, the viewer stands before a block of contradictions when, for instance, he chisels the words "Ich" and "Du" ("I" and "Thou") on opposite sides of a high pile of slightly curved concrete blocks. As a result of the impossible combination realized by the image, the viewer senses the absent body of the other in the intimate space of their own.

It is possible to be even more minimal, traced back even further to the essence. The neon *Eat/Death* (1972) by Bruce Nauman, in which the green letters "Eat" light up in the blue for "Death," is perhaps the ultimate compression of word and image, body and space, material and observation. With no more than two words intertwined with each other, the cycle of life and the material conditions that limit bodily existence are represented: death becomes eating becomes death and so on. As a silent, detached sculpture on the wall, it moreover offers the spectator room to reflect about the space of existence itself, between eating and dying. The compact neon is a mirror that confronts – and the verbal image, a realistic representation.

This example makes it clear that the figure of the human body has never truly been away (or, rather, has rapidly returned after minimalism) in contemporary sculpture. The fact that it is possible to represent it with just words, too, without direct figuration, is ironic for an art in which the word was traditionally absent. It proves, though, that sculpture continues to use that age-old tension as a vital driving force. Language and body: what is absent remains present, too, and what is invisible is exactly what art brings to light. The options have just expanded. Jenny Holzer has continued to make word sculptures since her *Truisms* (1977–1979) and *Inflammatory Essays* (1979–1982), in public spaces, on posters, billboards, skyscrapers, with projections or digital displays. And Juan Muñoz wrote even stories and made soundworks that give his narrative and figurative sculptures an extra dimension. That should not surprise us, either. Was not the golem already a figure of clay that came to life via the use of letters?

Language as interface

The silently sitting figures sculpted by Jaume Plensa from letters also belong to that lineage, as an expression of a tension between language, materiality, and thought which dominates contemporary life. It is telling that you cannot just look at his high figures on public squares, such as *White Nomad* (2021), with all their entangled diverse alphabets, as unreadable as they are melodious. You can also go stand in their bodies. It is as if for a moment you can just pull back into the contemplative stillness that they envelop and protect with their bodies, so as to look at all the squabbling and bustling babel in the public surroundings from that perspective, as in the silent eye of the storm. On the one hand, this kind of sculpture invites the spectator to stand literally in the mental space of the other. That is why its contours are transparent, like mesh for looking through the mix of cultural languages. On the other hand, the wrought-iron latticework makes the viewer also conscious of the need for stillness and detached observation, however instantaneous, to achieve an encounter and exchange of perspectives. For Plensa, stillness seems to be the precondition for understanding and dialogue.

That is no easy task, though, at a time in which the increase in means of communication and transportation has democratized the chances for encountering people from different languages and cultures, to be sure, but has also accelerated to such a degree that the real encounter often fails. Where does any space for dialogue prevail in our post-globalizing world? Where is any willingness to listen for the other's perspective in a time that allows its attention to be dictated by social media, with their continuous commands to represent yourself and their pressures to believe that only 'what is seen' really exists? It is no coincidence that the chiaroscuro drawings in which Plensa seems to have primarily imagined his language figures, have titles like *Stress* (2012) and *Insomnia* (2012).

Language is a skin that makes contact possible, an interface, yet just like the body, it is also a source of unspeakable isolation, a prison – the "mortal coil" that made Hamlet sigh "words, words, words." The *Hermit* (2012) that Plensa makes is enveloped by a meditative stillness, with hands over its raised knees like an ancient Cycladic statue, but the figure is also placed in isolation, on an solitary island of stone. Where he puts several versions together in a group, you see a blissful emptiness in and around them, yet also the unbridgeable distance that separates them, an incapacity to get in touch.

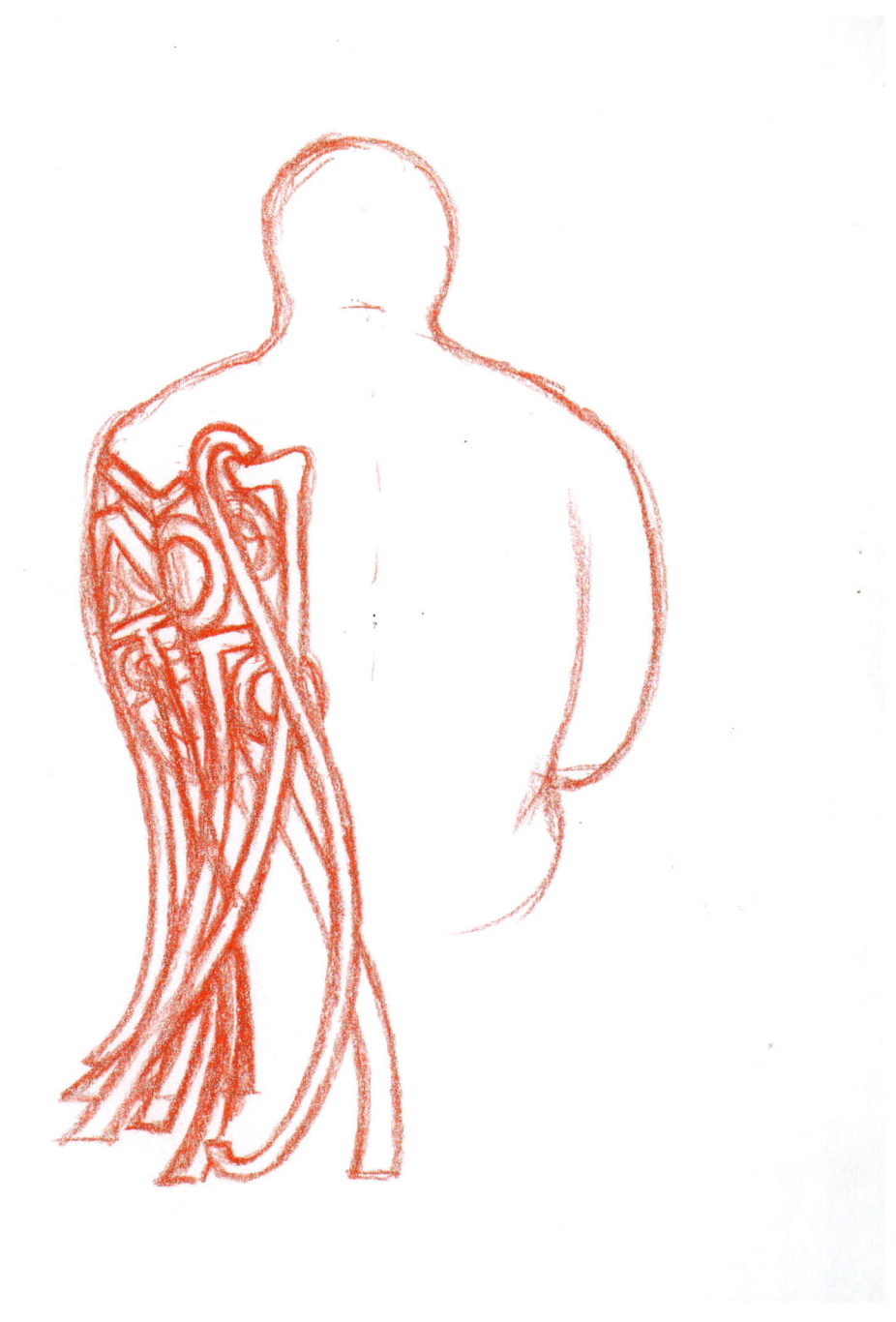

For sometimes words say nothing. That is why it is significant that Plensa raises his visual language from multilingual and multiform letters, the elemental material with which words become visible – as concrete as they are symbolic. In *Sculpture and Language* (2020), his inaugural address for the Collège de France from 2013, the sculptor Tony Cragg writes:

> Language is itself (as is human thought and emotion) a phenomenon of the material world. Every word or term that we have in our heads has been forged out of the material world into the common currency of symbols [...]. The relationship between language and material is integral and inseparable. Artworks are material entities and therefore must have language associated with them. Artworks become artworks because artists create things that bundle symbols together in a material form that expresses specific qualities and meanings. The tight relationship between material, language and thought enables artists to change the material forms and thereby create new thoughts and emotions. This essential and important relationship is the fundament of sculpture and what makes it into a powerful and relevant form or artistic expression.[7]

What Plensa makes visible with his characteristic sculptures is that language in its diversity is an elemental material that both envelops and crushes, opens and closes, divides and connects human beings. Yet the emotion and reflection that he calls forth has to do with the invisible material that intersects sculpture and language, body and space: stillness. It explains why his art sometimes reads like an hommage to the other art that puts stillness under tension: music. In *Heart of Trees* (2007), for example, bronze statues with the names of famous composers tattooed on their bodies sit, reticent and solitary, with their arms and legs around a tree, terrestrially rooted and at the same time ethereally oriented toward the music of the spheres.

Yet the embracing stillness inside and outside Plensa's sculptures makes his work, above all, untimely. In *Alienation and Acceleration* (2010), the German sociologist Hartmut Rosa writes that modernity is characterized by an acceleration that increasingly compresses space, almost making it contract. In that respect, Plensa's sculpture offers an antidote of the sort that Rosa advocates for. With his material language as both a skin and an interface between the stillness within his sculptural bodies and the body of the viewer, Plensa creates a space for resonance.

Notes

1   Alberto Giacometti, *Why I Am a Sculptor* (Paris: Éditions Fondation Giacometti & Editions Hermann, 2017), 21. Original citation from Alberto Giacometti, "La voiture démystifiée", *Arts* 639 (1957): 9–15.
2   "Niet de illusie van het reële, maar het reële zelf wordt geproduceerd (...)." Philip Van Isacker, *De Sculptura. Beschouwingen over beeldhouwkunst* (Ghent: Grafische Cel, 2017), 16.
3   "Zolang het lichaam de zetel is van het menselijke denken en voelen, zal de beeldhouwkunst, als medium dat naar het elementair menselijke probeert te graven, steeds opnieuw het lichaam als haar onderwerp gebruiken." Idem, 250.
4   "de behoefte die telkens weer ervaren wordt om het denken en voelen te comprimeren in een beeld." Idem, 17.
5   "niet alleen drager is van het rationele aspect, maar ook van de totaliteit van het menselijke, en omdat het zoveel verschillende voorstellingen toelaat als het zijn van de mens zelf complexiteit vertoont." Ibid.
6   For a clarification of how the sculpture creates "a new appearance from its incomplete shape" ("uit zijn onvolmaakte vorm een nieuw aanschijn") in Rilke's gaze, see also Paul Claes, "Het voorbeeldige gedicht. Over *Archaïscher torso Apollos*," *Raster* 82 (1998): 14–18.
7   Tony Cragg, *Sculpture and Language* (London: Galerie Thaddaeus Ropac, 2020), 13.

Literature cited

Claes, Paul. "Het voorbeeldige gedicht. Over *Archaïscher torso Apollos.*" *Raster* 82 (1998): 14–18.
Cragg, Tony. *Sculpture and Language*, London: Galerie Thaddaeus Ropac, 2020.
Giacometti, Alberto. *Why I Am a Sculptor*. Translated by Catherine Petit and Paul Buck. Paris: Éditions Fondation Giacometti & Éditions Hermann, 2017.
Rosa, Hartmut. *Leven in tijden van versnelling. Een pleidooi voor resonantie*, translated by Huub Stegemann. Amsterdam: Boom Uitgevers, 2016.
Van Isacker, Philip. *De sculptura. Beschouwingen over beeldhouwkunst*. Ghent: Grafisch Cel, LUCA School of Arts, 2017.

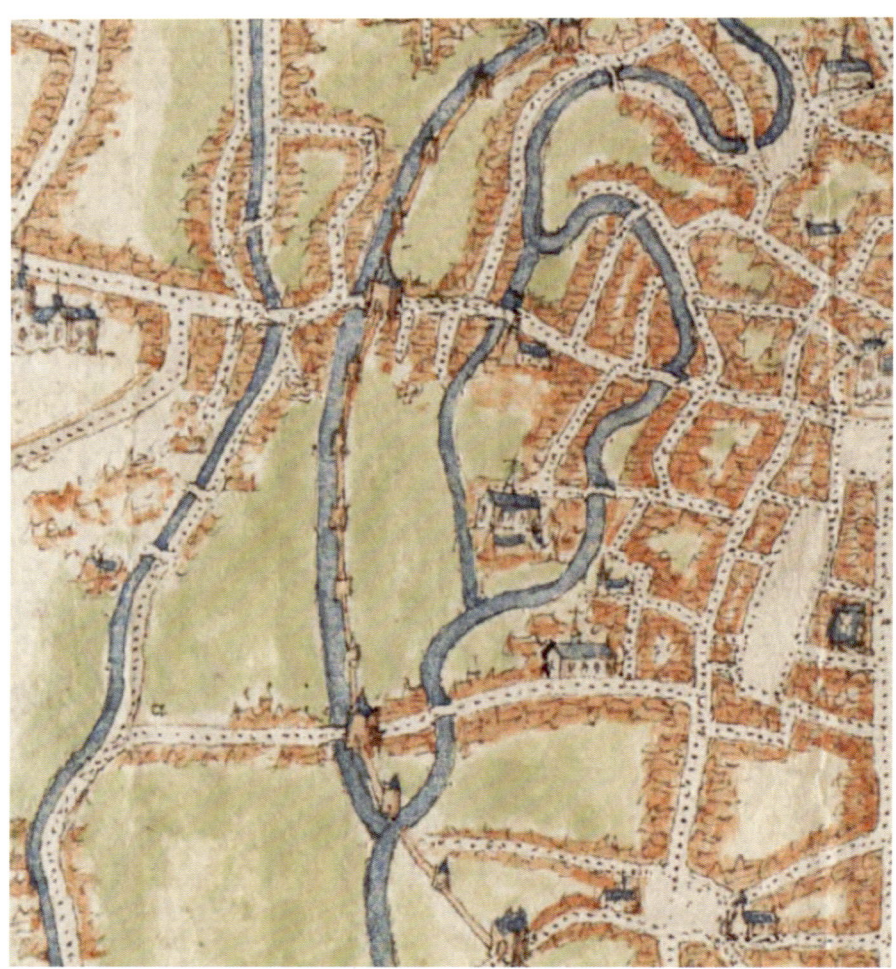

Detail of the map of Leuven, Jacob van Deventer, 1550.

St. Raphaël's Square

Rebecca Gysen & Karen Landuydt

A new site, which combines original environmental features with modern urban development is currently being developed, right at the very crossroads of the Dyle River and Leuven's medieval centre. A whole new district is being built on a true heritage site, adding greenery to it, next to an exposed Dyle River, different types of housing, commercial spaces, and cultural hot spots.

This site is historically so unique because of the intertwining of the history of Leuven with its university's history. From the thirteenth century onwards up until very recently people were being cared for at the intersection of the Dyle valley and Brusselsestraat. This important public role was complemented by the university's lectures on medicine and healthcare. Therefore, the healthcare site which arose on this very spot was not only a physical crossroad but also an important societal crossroad.

Nowadays, Gasthuisberg has become the premium healthcare site of Leuven, but the straight axis connecting this modern healthcare site, built upon a hill just outside Leuven, with the city centre crosses right through the historical healthcare site downtown, along with all its traces of a rich past.

Therefore, we can say that Plensa's piece of art is placed on a unique intersection between past and present between a rural landscape and cityscape between university and town.

The early days of healthcare in Leuven
St. Elisabeth's *gasthuis*

In Leuven, the first *gasthuis* (a comprehensive healthcare centre for that time) was erected between 1090–1095, close to the future St Jacob's Church. When constructing the city wall in 1156, this *gasthuis* ended up located outside of it. Henry I, duke of Brabant, donated part of his property – which was located within the borders of the town wall – for the construction of a new *gasthuis*, built around 1222.

This thirteenth-century hospital housed 18 beds for the ill and a chapel. A more detailed description of the *gasthuis* is not preserved.

The original *gasthuis* functioned as a haven of refuge for travellers, pilgrims, and the poor. The hospital was served by both friars and nuns. From the second half of the thirteenth century onwards, however the nuns took on this responsibility solely, albeit without strict monastic rules. Over time, city council authority grew. By 1390, the *gasthuis* housed 25 beds, and this number kept on growing steadily throughout the centuries. Noble families and prominent citizens supported the hospital by donating land, pasture, forests, tenant farms, as well as by financing hospital beds. This support also led to the acquisition of the land on which, many years later (during the twentieth century), the state-of-the-art, very modern hospital complex Gasthuisberg would arise.

During the late fifteenth century, the authorities intervened on account of conflicts with the nuns, accused of overmuch worldly behaviour. The hospital was erected under the supervision of Nikolaas Hellens, a professor at Leuven University. In 1479, he initiated a reorganization, put the finances back in order, and installed a community of Augustine nuns.

Thanks to several donations during the first half of the sixteenth century, the hospital was renovated, including the addition of a new chapel and a convent. A series of devastating fires hit the hospital in 1632 and again in 1718; subsequently followed by a renovation in the second half of the eighteenth century including the redesign of various interiors.

During the French regime at the end of the eighteenth century, the convent community was abolished and the St. Elisabeth's *gasthuis* became public property. The nuns however continued to provide healthcare.

Nowadays the Romaanse Poort, is the only thirteenth-century building still standing on-site. Remnants of the chapel walls were found right beneath the current chapel, which was erected in the sixteenth century.

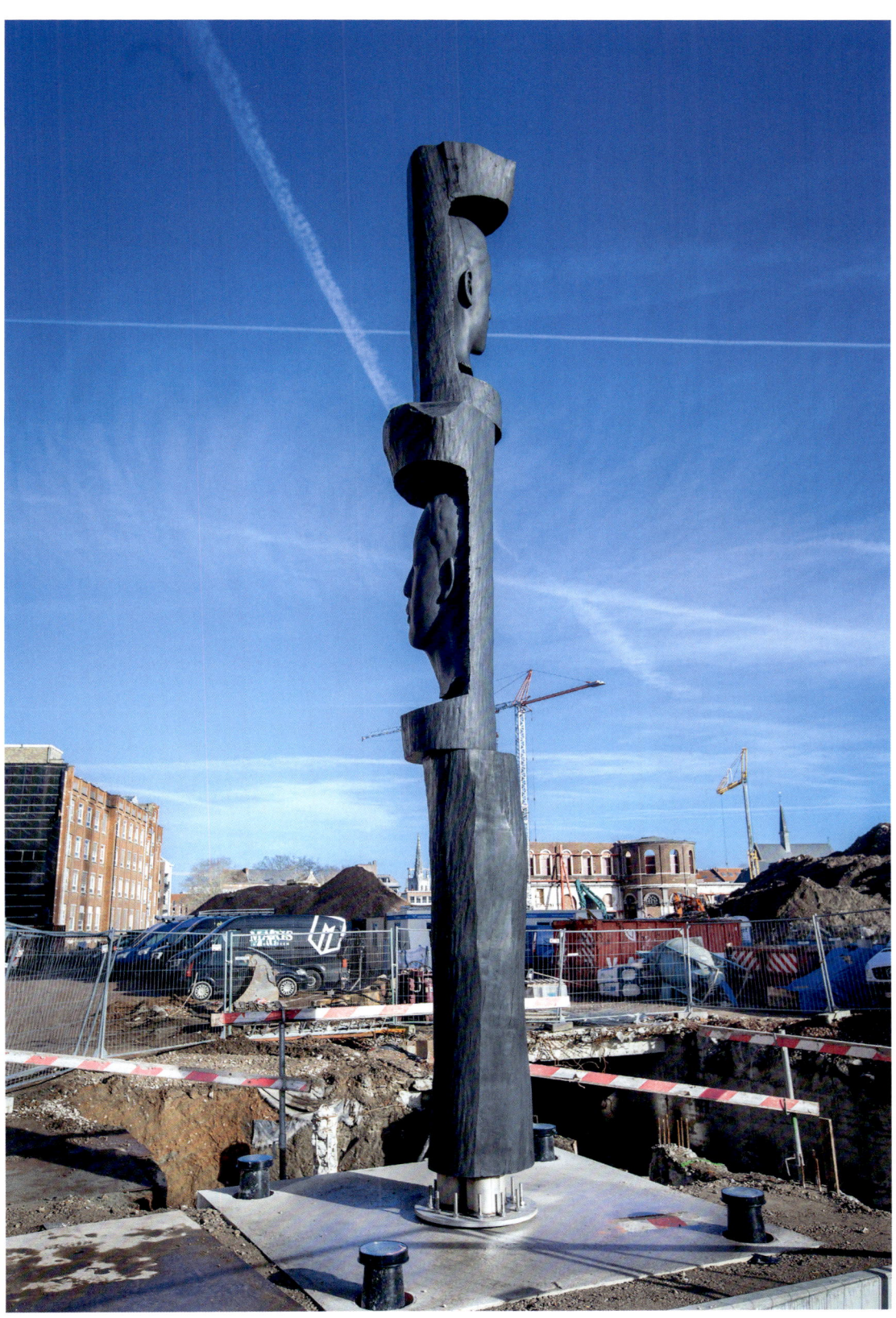

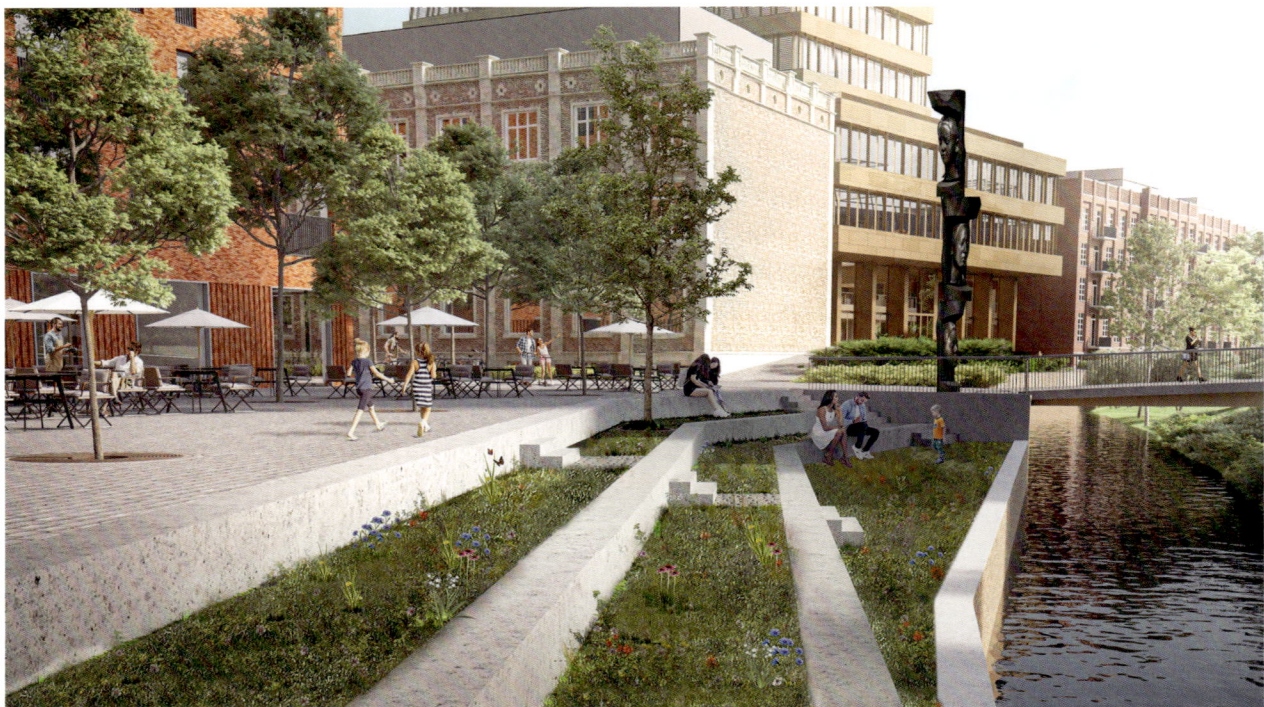

Rendering of the location for *The Four Elements* after completion of the site.

The early days of the medicine faculty
The anatomical amphitheatre

The official inauguration of Leuven's university took place on September 7, 1426. This also announced the erection of a Faculty of Medicine. Initially, future physicians received an education in the liberal arts, followed by four years of subsequent training, later shortened to three years. Classes were held in two halls of the *Lakenhalle* (Cloth Hall).

Students were enrolled in two courses: one course oriented towards "illnesses and their treatment" and one course oriented towards "anatomy, physiology, and hygiene". Medical training was primarily theoretical. It is not entirely clear whether anatomical demonstrations were already being performed at the time.

We know that classes in botany were also being offered. The classes for this subject were seasonal and took place outdoors around the area of the city walls or in the convent gardens. The first mention of an anatomical class in Leuven dissecting the human body dates from 1533, lectured by doctor Andreas Vesalius.

An important milestone for development of the medical campus on this site came in 1738, when the Faculty of Medicine purchased a piece of land on the corner of the Minderbroederstraat and the Kapucijnenvoer. On these premises – originally property of the Van Ophem family – a landscaped garden including a pond, a brook, a bridge, and a pavilion could be found. It was at this very spot that the university set up its first *Kruidtuin*, a garden for scientific botanical and medical research. In 1744, an idea coined by physician and professor Hendrik Jozef Rega, an anatomical amphitheatre was erected up these premises. It served as a classroom for anatomical experiments reflecting the scientific progress within medical science at the time, which had recognized the importance of practice-based research since the sixteenth century, led by Vesalius.

During the French regime, not only the monasteries and convents were abolished, but the university as well. The revolutionary authorities installed new institutions, including two healthcare institutions: a Commission for *Burgerlijke Godshuizen*, oriented towards healthcare and assistance and the *Bureel van Weldadigheid*, responsible for reducing poverty, both forerunners of the future OCMW (i.e., a public centre for social welfare). The Commission for *Burgerlijke Godshuizen* acquired possession of St. Elisabeth's *gasthuis* in 1809.

During the Dutch regime (1815–1830), the *Rijksuniversiteit* was established, which oversaw the medical operations of St. Elisabeth's from 1817 onwards. In the meantime, the hospital was expanded with specialized rooms for medical care, such as a delivery room and a room for those with terminal illnesses. Nuns still continued to provide healthcare. The university used this hospital for the clinical research of its medicine students.

St. Peter's Hospital

In 1830, the Commission for Civil Hospitals concluded that St. Elisabeth's *gasthuis* no longer met nineteenth-century hygienic standards. More natural light and ventilation were needed, as well as room to effectively quarantine patients.

In 1838 a convention between the Catholic University – re-established in Leuven in 1834–1835 – and the City of Leuven led to the decision of building a new hospital, St. Peter's Hospital. It was architect Alexander Van Arenbergh who designed a monumental rectangular building with two inner courtyards, four pavilions, and a large garden, in which approximately 250 patients could be hospitalized. Men and women were in separate halls with no less than 24 beds each. This hospital – property of the Commission – also functioned as an academic hospital and was the most important training site for medicine students at Leuven University.

The Vesalius Institute

Meanwhile, the anatomical amphitheatre at the site mentioned above had become outdated and unsuitable. In 1876–1877, the re-established Catholic University had Joris Helleputte design the Vesalius Institute. This institute comprised an octagonal auditorium for 200 students and a rectangular dissection hall. The institute was directly connected to St. Peter's Hospital on Brusselsestraat.

The Vesalius Institute – considered a model institution upon its inauguration – was a historical milestone for the further development of the Catholic University of Leuven, most importantly for its Faculty of Medicine. It symbolized the start of an intensive building policy that lasted until World War I, driven by a growing student population and increasing scientific activities. It served as an 'extension' of St. Peter's Hospital, where students received their practical training. It was the first step in the systematic expansion of a fully-fledged medicine campus.

Around 1900, the growing number of students compelled St. Peter's Hospital to carry out further extension projects, whereby the above-mentioned *hortus* largely had to make way for the construction of clinical auditoria. The advent of bacteriology – a new specialization – demanded investments in laboratories, sterilization chambers, bandaging rooms, and improved operating rooms. During the first half of the twentieth century, this nineteenth-century edifice was exposed to constant alterations influenced by medical progress.

In 1930, a first attempt at a more structural solution was carried out. Brussels-based architect Gustave Maukers presented a plan to add an entire storey and to divide the rooms in the building. During the Interbellum Maukers belonged to a group of architects who tried to modernize hospital architecture, focusing on the intended functions of rooms. Mauker's plan provided rooms suitable for pediatric medicine, pulmonology, and dermatology, among others. As opposed to Ghent and Brussels this functionalism would only be partially realized in Leuven before World War II.

The origins of St. Raphaël's Campus
The Cancer Institute

During the interbellum a second campus arose on the very same site: St. Raphaël's Hospital, running parallel with the development of St. Peter's Hospital. This was necessary, as the St. Peter's Hospital could no longer fulfill the new scientific and educational needs, neither keep up with the university's growing student population.

The first institute on this campus was the Maisin 'Cancer Institute', established in 1927 by Professor Joseph Maisin, who specialized in bacteriology, anatomo-pathology, and oncology. This institute was the first of its kind in Belgium and gained international recognition for its groundbreaking research and for its use of advanced techniques in cancer treatment. In subsequent years, four more hospitals were established on the same site: a surgical clinic, a maternity clinic, a clinic for internal medicine and, lastly, a pediatric clinic in 1937.

The creation of the Cancer Institute gave rise to the establishment of a School of Nursing. The university came to an agreement with Sisters of Charity in Ghent to take over the existing nursing school in the Naamsestraat and to establish it. Shortly after the arrival of the first Sisters of Charity in 1928, it was decided to build a new cloister and school along the aforementioned Kapucijnenvoer. The chapel was consecrated in 1934. Student nurses were engaged for healthcare until the seventies.

All these new clinics and institutes gave rise to the development of new medical specialties. This growth was also strengthened by another dynamic: *vernederlandsing* ('Dutchification'), whereby originally non-Dutch-language classes shifted to using Dutch. The number of disciplines taught in Dutch, however, grew slowly. More patients were needed in order to eliminate redundancies in Dutch and French taught clinical courses in the Faculty of Medicine.

As a result, an amalgam of academic clinics arose on this site by the end of the thirties. World War II was a horrible period causing much damage. Plans for reconstruction and expansion were being made, focussing more on centralisation and integration, yet starting from the idea of sanitary vision, as the idea of splitting up wasn't explored at the time.

After the war, the fate of the 'old' St. Peter's Hospital seemed sealed, given the enormous damage caused by the war. In 1946, the Commission for Public Welfare (COO) – a merger of the Commission for *Burgerlijke*

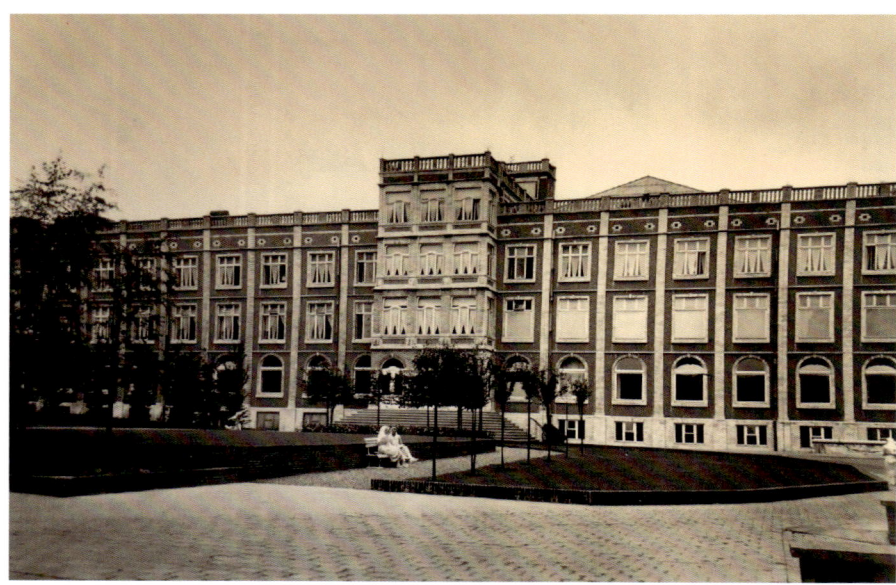

Façade of the prestigious Cancer Institute

Godshuizen and the *Bureel van Weldadigheid* in consultation with university representatives decided to build a new hospital. Financial resources were available thanks to reconstruction funds as well as national funds for hospital construction in the fifties. Tearing down the old building and reconstructing new one seemed the most obvious choice. The design by the architectural trio Cloquet-Van Montfort-Vandeput was approved in 1951. Demolition began immediately, after and four years later the first wing of the new St. Peter's Hospital arose, a fourteen-storey high-rise building.

Architecturally, the first part of this new hospital structure was more modern, including centralization of shared departments (radiology, intensive care, administration, etc.) and a separation of visitors, patients, and medical staff flows. Only the renovated nineteenth-century south wing of St. Peter's Hospital was preserved.

In order to better connect both hospitals (of St. Peter's and St. Raphaël's), projects such as a central heating facility and the enclosure of the Dyle River were realized. In the second half of the 1960s, an emergency centre was opened up at the backside of the hospital, where ambulances drove in and out via the Brusselsestraat, across the covered Dyle River.

As a consequence of the heavy financing of academic clinics, among other causes, the resentment between the COO and the university gradually increased, which resulted in quite a lot of construction delay. The language conflict also escalated throughout the course of 1960s, which ultimately led to the separation of het medical departments of the university. This resulted in a new, academic hospital in Sint-Lambrechts-Woluwe (near Brussels), run by a staff of the French speaking community. By this time, the Leuven Hospitals were completely 'dutchified.'

A master plan from 1967 formulated two fundamental objectives for the long term: on the one hand, there should come a shift towards a centralization and an integration of the scattered and outdated research and educational facilities on a new site, meant to bring forth a highly specialized university hospital which replace the old-fashioned St. Raphaël's hospital. On the other hand, the expansion of St. Peter's Hospital as a regional hospital should be a main priority. At the beginning of the 1970s, this master plan would be further refined. Emphasis came to be on the creation of an organic entity made up of complementary hospitals, ruling on mutual competition.

The decision to create further unity between the various clinics in St. Raphaël's resulted in the construction of a large high-rise building, which was completed in November 1973.

The original plan to build multiple high-rise buildings on the same location, however, was superseded as a result of rapid evolution in the hospital sector. The flexibility to keep up with the fast-moving developments within medical science and technology lacked within the St. Raphaël complex. This compelled the building of another new hospital complex, one which would also ensure further growth of the Dutch-speaking Faculty of Medicine in Leuven.

At the same time, Dutch-speaking professors decided to expand their activities beyond the city centre. The first stone for the Gasthuisberg campus was laid in the early seventies. The children's hospital – which was the first of many buildings on-site – opened its doors In 1974–1975.

In hindsight the decision to keep investing in St. Peter's hospital proved to be a mistake. A second a new wing was inaugurated in 1977. Another large new edifice was erected in the early eighties, a building of which, unfortunately, only a few floors have been actually used. In the meantime, policies changed: there exist a national "excess of beds" and there was a need for savings. Expensive and partially unused, St. Peter's Hospital became a sensitive issue in the relationship between the city and the university. A 'love-hate' relationship quickly emerged between the city of Leuven and this high-rise building. On the one hand, it was a place where many citizens of Leuven were born (this brought back happy memories); on the other hand, it was a place with a massive unwieldy edifice set up, which constituted a scar in the city's medieval and historical town centre, and even acquired the nickname "the yellow elephant."

From an isolated island in the city to a new, sustainable district in the Dyle River valley

Ever since the 1980s this hospital site had thus been a crowded heavily built on site, right in the middle of the city, enclosed by the thoroughfares of the Brusselsestraat, Kapucijnenvoer, and Minderbroederstraat, resulting in some sort of 'island in the city'. Despite many historically valuable buildings still present on site, this location primarily served as a utilitarian place which barely entered into a relationship with the urban surroundings. Moreover, it was a site which was being phased out, and time was needed to develop a vision for its future.

Over the years, many conceptual exercises were made in order to define a useful purpose of this site. It was only in 2014 that a mutually agreed upon masterplan between the university and the city had been approved. The site acquired the name "Hertogen site," referring to the name of the "Hertogen island" where the origins of the hospital site lie.

One of the points of departure for this masterplan is that new building blocks will be formed, which will time and again embrace and give meaning to the valuable historical buildings which refer to the site's rich past. Although much needs to be demolished in order to "refresh" the site which had been paved over throughout the years, the masterplan foresees preserving a good amount of "silent witnesses" of a rich healthcare past on-site anyhow.

In addition, the scenery of the Dyle River valley will be quit essential in the design of the new city district. For years, the Dyle River has been covered, yet in the future it will be opened up again, bringing about more greenery. A modern-day vision for urban development will be implemented on this site, a vision with a special focus on so-called "blue" and "green" areas. By doing so the "island" in the Dyle River will become "liveable" again. This time however, without an isolating effect, as the new city district will enter into a relationship with its direct surroundings. It will be connected with its neighbouring districts and streets via bridges and paths oriented towards pedestrians and cyclists. The principles of "proximity in the city" will be applied, sustainable travel behaviour will be encouraged, and motorized vehicles will be banned as much as possible in order to create a pleasant and safe public space.

The ideas laid out in the masterplan (dating back to late sixties and early seventies) concerning a "split healthcare offer" are only preserved partially. The university opted to abandon the site for the most part, yet it would like to preserve the last bit standing of St. Raphaël's high-rise building and convert this into a Wellness Tower offering many wellness and healthcare services to the citizens. Furthermore, the site will primarily function as a residential area offering several types of housing next to all kinds of shops and restaurants. In addition to this, the site will also comprise two or two brand new major cultural hubs, serving both the city and the university.

The Performing Arts site, where the historical and the innovative city meet

The City of Leuven decided to further elaborate the cultural component currently already present on the Augustinian Sisters Convent site in the Brusselsestraat, turning it into a brand new, state-of-the-art, Performing Arts Centre. Via an open call from the Flemish Government Architect, an international design team led by Sergison Bates architects was appointed. This team surprised everyone with a comprehensive and clear-cut vision, based on the original masterplan for the Hertogen site. The new building will be incorporated in such a way that it will allow the remnants of the convent to "shine on" after years of predominance of the "yellow elephant", as the convent was severely hit-during the erection of St. Peter's hospital in the nineteenth century and therefor some somewhat neglected. Abiding by the modern trends and architecture, the entire site will be connected with the very centre via the nearby Brusselsestraat, an old medieval gateway.

Moreover, the third branch of the Dyle River, flowing right through the site, regains its important role as a key element in the urban landscape.

The city's main objective for this new, innovative city quarter is to really "live" its slogan "Samen stad maken" ("Creating city together") on this historically so important site.

In 2020, after years of vacancy, St. Peter's Hospital (on the Brusselsestraat) was demolished. While awaiting the realization of the new Performing Arts Centre, the freed-up, vacant land has been occupied by the artwork *Velodroom* and recently transformed into the Olevodroom. These temporary art installations help to already experiment with the concept of "Samen stad maken" and, at the same time, helps to add the site and its new destination to the mental map of Leuven's residents.

Plensa at the Hertogen site

At the other far end of the Hertogen site, the university, decided to establish an innovative museum, centred on the historical figure of Vesalius, yet encompassing future-oriented view on the human body and medical science.

This way, the anatomical theatre designed by Joris Helleputte as well as the range of historical buildings surrounding it, located on Minderbroederstraat, can durably serve as a silent witness of its rich healthcare past. At the same time, this site can become a showcase of innovation about healthcare and wellness, stimulated by university research.

It is right in the middle of all these crossroads (between city and university, between history and innovation, between rural scenery and urbanization), that Plensa's new artwork will be placed. It will add meaning to this valuable site and to the unbreakable bond between the city of Leuven and its famous university.

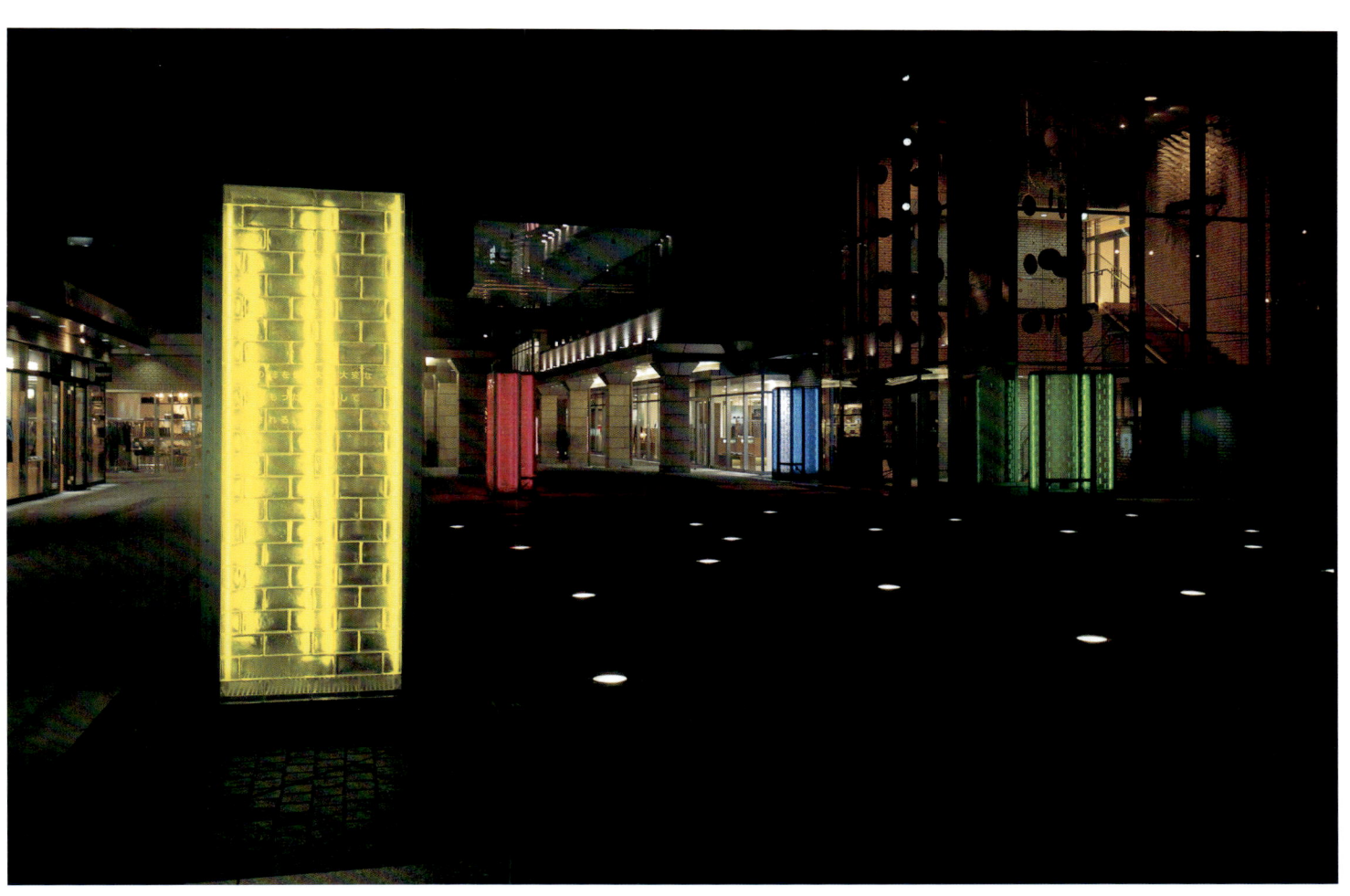

Literature cited

De Cock, Paul, Kenis, Ramon, Swiggers Pierre en Van Vlasselaer, Michel. "Ontwikkelingsgeschiedenis Hertogensite" in Nieuwsbrief Leuvens Historisch Genootschap, 2023–2024

In goede handen: 75 jaar onderwijs verpleeg- en vroedkunde in Leuven. Leuven, 2004.

Nys, Liesbet. *Van mensen en muizen. Vijftig jaar Nederlandstalige faculteit geneeskunde aan de Leuvense universiteit*, Leuven, 2016.

Vandendriessche, Joris. *Zorg en Wetenschap: een geschiedenis van de Leuvense academische ziekenhuizen in de twintigste eeuw.* Leuven, 2019.

Verbruggen, Herman. *Gezondheidszorg in het oude Leuven: een wandelgids*, Leuven, 2009.

KU Leuven, Faculteit Geneeskunde. "Ons rijke verleden." https://med.kuleuven.be/nl/over-ons/geschiedenis

UZ Leuven. "Geschiedenis UZ Leuven." https://www.uzleuven.be/nl/over-ons/investeren-de-toekomst/pioniersmentaliteit/geschiedenis-uz-leuven

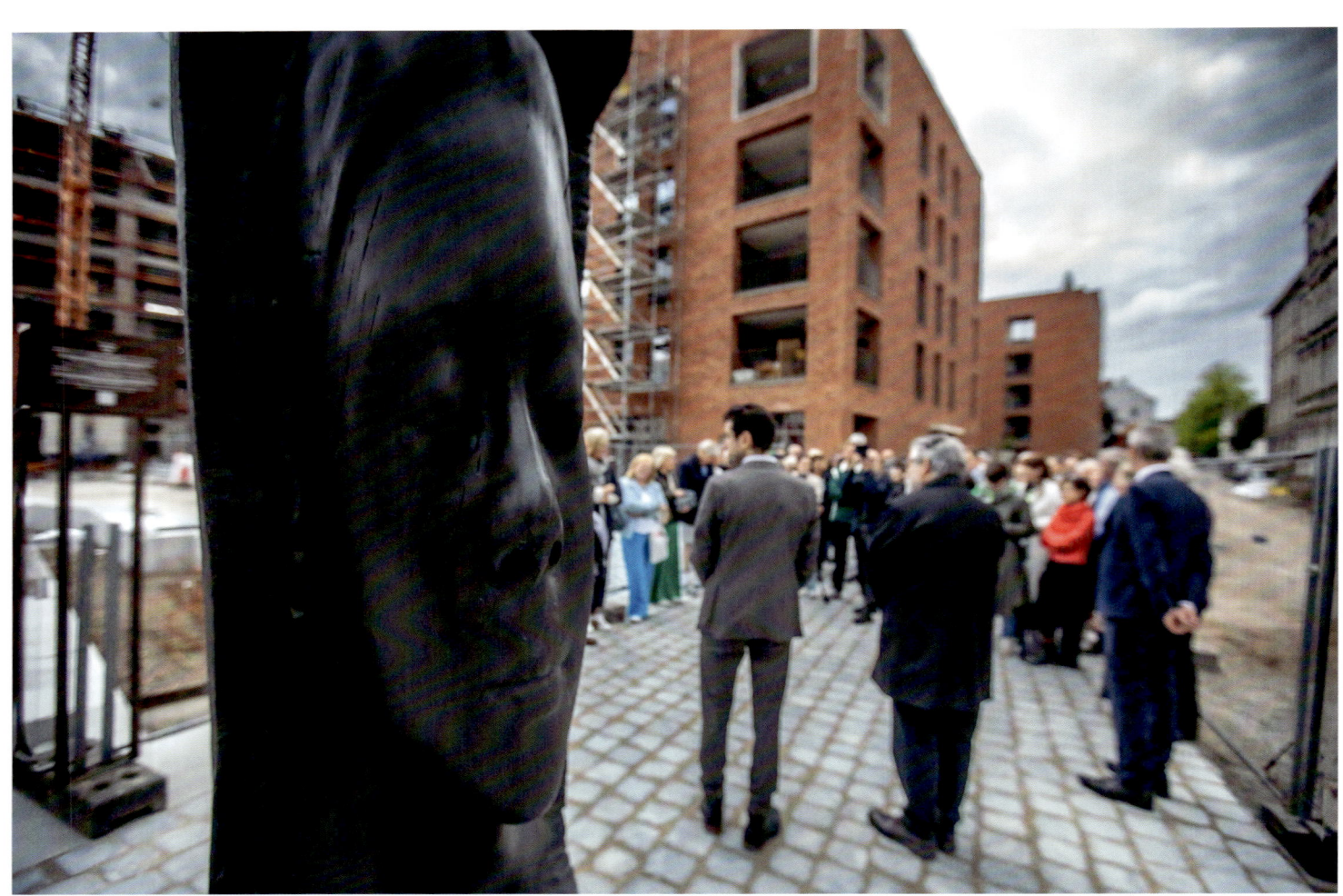

Leuven: Art in Public Spaces

Stéfanie Lambrechts

By means of introduction

High upon his bluestone pedestal, *Justus Lipsius* looks out over the avenue named Bondgenotenlaan. On the Oude Markt square, another landmark sculpture called *De Kotmadam* awaits the next tourist who wants to be in the photo, while *De Fiere Margriet* iconically floats upstream on the Dyle River. With its medieval streets and modern squares, the city center of Leuven counts quite a number of legendary statues and monuments – 92 of them, to be precise.[1] They originate from a time when art primarily served to recall significant events or honor illustrious rulers. The majority of these sculptures are therefore monuments for commemorating the World Wars or important men on pedestals. First in line was the co-founder of the Belgian state, Sylvain Van de Weyer (1876), as Leuven's response to the royal decree of January 7, 1835, which prescribed honoring the memory of "the Belgians who had contributed to the glory of their fatherland."[2]

Today, these historical sculptures blend into the streetscape, barely visible to passersby. Yet, they characterize Leuven as a bustling center for culture and heritage, revealing a glimpse of the city's rich history. "They make us reflect on the otherness of the past and, by doing so, of the future as well."[3]

Just as these statues are symbols for their moment in time, artworks placed in public spaces today will tell our descendants something about our present society and worldview. Maybe Jaume Plensa's *The Four Elements* will remind them of the synergy between science and art in Leuven or of the university's centuries-old presence as an essential corner stone of Leuven's DNA.

Art and urban space

In 2024 A.D., (urban) society has fundamentally changed. In line with other Flemish cities, the number of inhabitants in Leuven remains on the rise. The pressure on available space, including the public domain, grows along with it. No collective space is more actively used than public space. By definition it is a shared place, a crossroad of different realities, contexts and backgrounds. At any given moment during the day, residents walk to the supermarket around the corner, youngsters meet up on a local square, students bike from their student housing to campus, grandparents accompany their grandchildren to school or a bike is being parked against the pedestal of, let's say, Pieter Coutereel.

The importance of a qualitative, urban space is therefore gaining more and more recognition. The recent pandemic has highlighted this again, as well as its crucial role in stimulating our mental and physical well-being. Over the past decades, policymakers and spatial planners prioritized improving the aesthetic quality and livability of this public domain. In Leuven, too, urban renewal projects followed one another at a rapid pace, such as the rebuild of Ladeuze Square and the neighborhood around the train station during the nineties or, more recently, the canal zone and Hertogen site.

Art can also be a significant contributor to the livability and social cohesion of public space. Today, artworks are no longer an unambiguous representation of personae or events, but instead address the spectator as a critically thinking individual. Inciting encounters, they enter into dialogue with the urban context and its inhabitants.

This insight developed from the seventies onwards – not coincidentally, a period in time during which policymakers were very enthusiastic about the idea of democratizing art. Even smaller Flemish municipalities started to have a local cultural or community center, which made that every Flemish person had access to cultural life within a stone's throw. Barriers

130

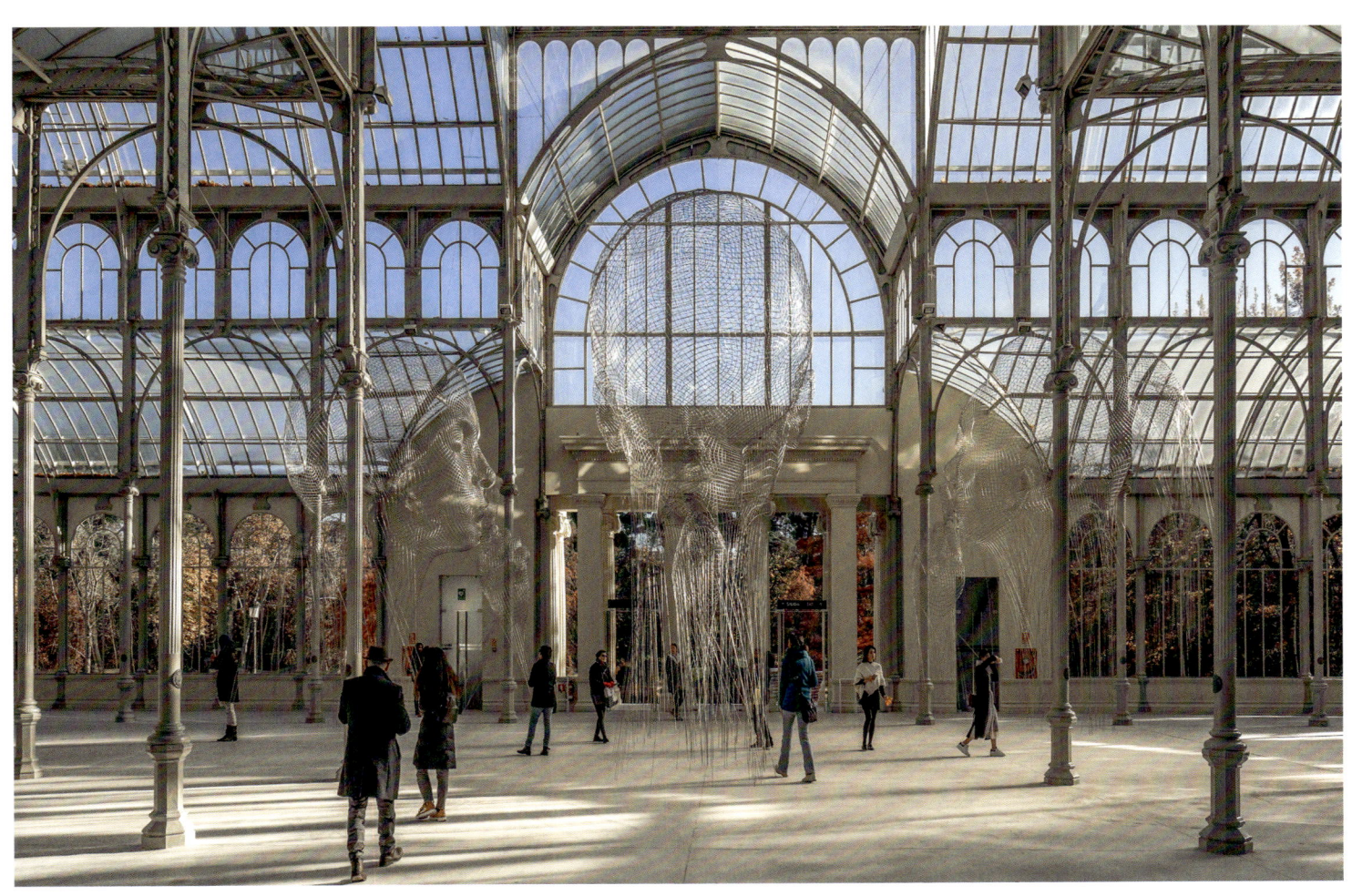

were lowered by bringing the visual arts into the public domain and by setting up participatory programs with local residents.

Art in public spaces is accessible to a broad, diverse, yet unpredictable public, a public that is not always familiar with looking at art. Reading a book, visiting an exhibition, or listening to a music album are all conscious choices. On the contrary, an artwork set up on, let's say, a roundabout, square or street, just 'happens' to us, without being obtrusive. Some passersby look at the artwork daily, – some passersby will ignore it completely and yet another category of passersby will thoroughly inspect it just once and maybe even taking it home by means of a picture for a photo album. The artwork in the public space balances between blending into its surroundings and commanding our attention in a cityscape full of sensory stimuli.

In other words, an artwork in the public space cannot fall back on the framework or conventions of a museum, which yields greater vulnerability for the workpiece of art itself and the artist. There is not a single artwork in the public space that remains untouched by criticism. It is subject to an everchanging society with varying value systems and interests of passersby. "[An artwork] has to be incorporated into space (whether harmoniously or not), has to conform to the conditions that that space imposes (location, accessibility, exposure to weather, damage, ...), *and* has to take into account all the different concerns and functions that come together in a public space: property interests, spatial planning, safety and health, social roles, economic purposes, etc."[4]

Despite this complexity, different artists – such as Jaume Plensa, Christo and Jeanne-Claude, or Antony Gormley – very consciously choose to create art especially for the public space. Perhaps because art in public spaces contributes to the unique identity of a city, and furthermore to a greater personal bond between an inhabitant and a local square or street. As an advisor for cities and municipalities in the area of art in public spaces, Arno van Roosmalen emphasizes the importance of meaningful spaces, creating opportunities for people to identify with that particular spot, for instance by means of the narrative it offers.

A site's narrative or its social function often constitutes the artist's starting point. Also, the future purpose of a certain area or street can give rise to a new piece of art. For this reason, art commissions in public spaces regularly usher in a site's transition. After all, an artwork can build a bridge between the past and the challenges of the future. This being said, Plensa's

The Four Elements on the Hertogen site not only constitutes a glimpse of a future city district with healthcare and cultural roles, but also the historical context of the site, which has been a social crossroads for the university and the city for centuries. In addition to this, the work formally refers to the medieval *Sedes Sapientiae*, a sculpture by Nicolaas De Bruyne (1442) in Leuven's St. Peter's Church.

Art as a driving force for reflection

By transcending the generic cityscape, art invites passersby to reflect and stand still. This invitation can be explicit, as with the recent artwork *Aedicula* by Renato Nicolodi (2023) on the site of Abdij van Park (Park Abbey), a Premonstratensian abbey, which invites for contemplation due to its solitary nature. The invitation can also be implicit, as in Plensa's work, which compels us to stop, pause and reflect not only as a result of its monumental proportions, but also as a result of its poetic force. It can put certain themes in the spotlight, such as identity and vulnerability to resonate and challenge us to take a stand.

Different than historical or folkloristic statues, art today succeeds in not propagating just one unequivocal meaning or message but instead in allowing different interpretations and opinions. This 'multi-layeredness' of art in public spaces contributes to the democratization of public space and to the creation of an inclusive and collective public space. Author of *The Emancipated Spectator*, Jacques Rancière, articulates it as follows: "the images of art help sketch new configurations of what can be seen, what can be said and what can be thought and, consequently a new landscape of the possible. But they do so on condition that their meaning or effect is not anticipated."[5]

Even though most artworks in public spaces are of a permanent nature, temporary artistic interventions nevertheless contribute to this democratization as well. They are able to react more rapidly to topical social issues, serving as an experiment in which societal dynamics and cultural identity are investigated or challenged. An example of this kind of response is the work *Go Away Sorrow of the World* by Frank&Robbert Robbert&Frank, which was part of the exhibition project titled *As You Think So Shall You Become* (2022) for STUK, the Leuven-based arts center. Or *Velodroom* at the Hertogen site by the artists Thuy and Herzeele which is an artistic cycling track that served as a temporary meeting spot for the neighborhood. In a subsequent phase, this artwork has been turned almost literally inside out by Decoratelier from Brussels. In this way, the public domain is transformed into a kind of laboratory for society, in which different perspectives are being explored.

Towards a future-proof collection

A summary report from the Flemish Department of Culture, Youth and Media (2022) showed that the implementation of a vision on art in public spaces is not a policy priority in most Flemish cities.[6] In the city of Leuven, too, art commissions in public spaces came about rather project-based, sporadically and often motivated by the neighborhood district, until quite recently. This approach, however, risks to "clutter" the public domain. Recent artworks such as *Oeratoom* by Félicie d'Estienne d'Orves (2021) or *Vlaggenmast* by Cas-co and 019 (2023) undeniably bring about much added value to the city of Leuven, though relate to other images and artworks only on account of their physical proximity. Hence, we can state that elaborating a vision for art in public spaces starts, therefore, with becoming aware of its totality.

Among other things, the Flemish Platform Kunst in Opdracht strongly advocates to think in terms of collections rather than an ad hoc way of thinking, whereby both historical and new artworks are considered from a holistic vision as a public museum collection.[7] According to Samuel Saelemakers, curator of the Collection Kunst in de Stad in Antwerp, thinking in terms of collections begins with taking care of what is present today: "If you don't care for what is currently existing, you cannot expect to yield support for something new overnight."[8] It is important to maintain, restore, unlock and most importantly, to list what exists currently. Therefore, a thorough retro-analysis of artworks present is therefore essential as an anchor point and sounding board for the further expansion of the art collection in public spaces. In 2022–2023, the art and architecture studio Gijs Van Vaerenbergh laid out an instructional lab with architecture students from KU Leuven, focusing on the historical collection of statues in Leuven's public spaces. In collaboration with the City Archive, they made a start for this inventory, and they made proposals for interventions that question the meaning of the sculptures: *statues revisited.*

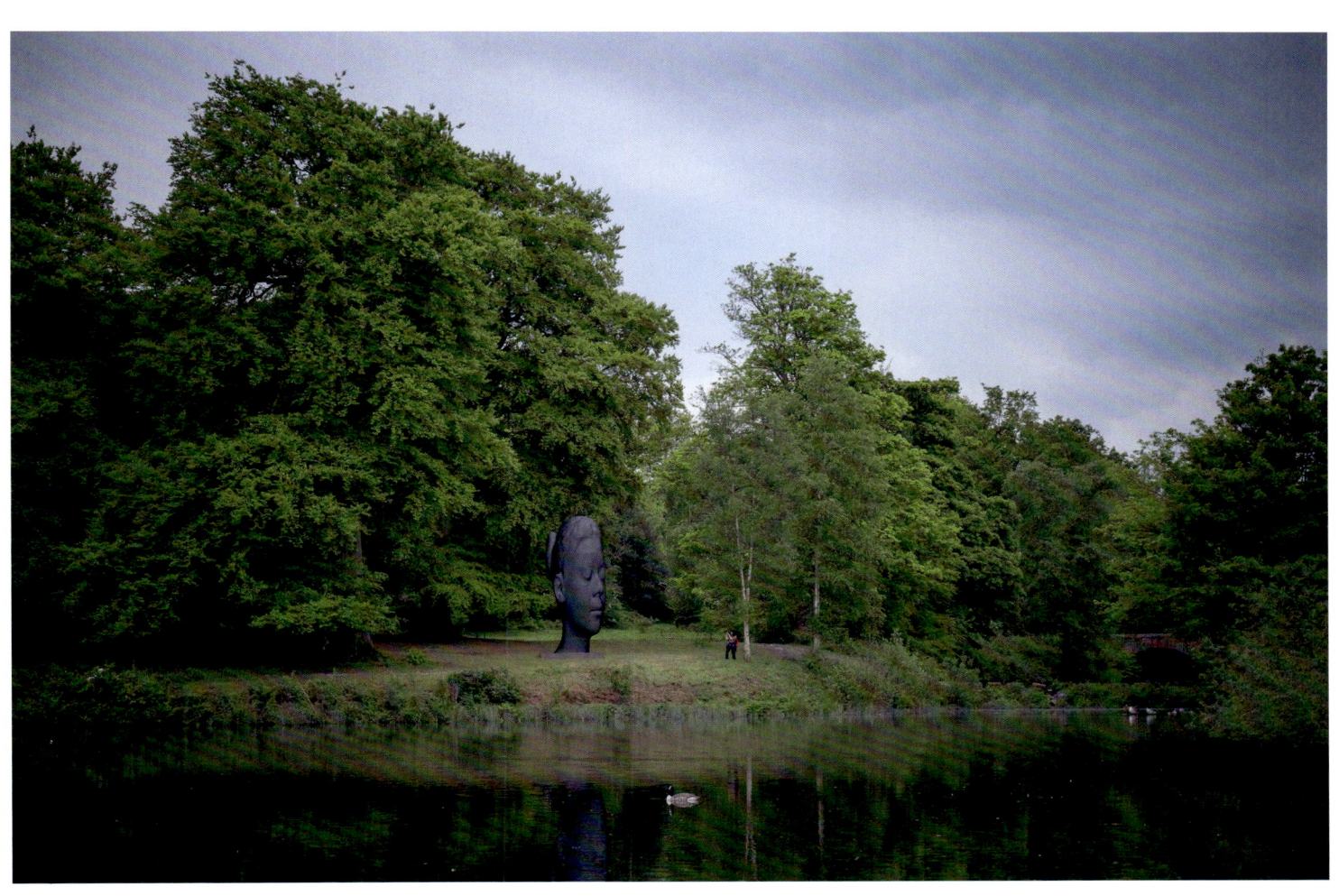

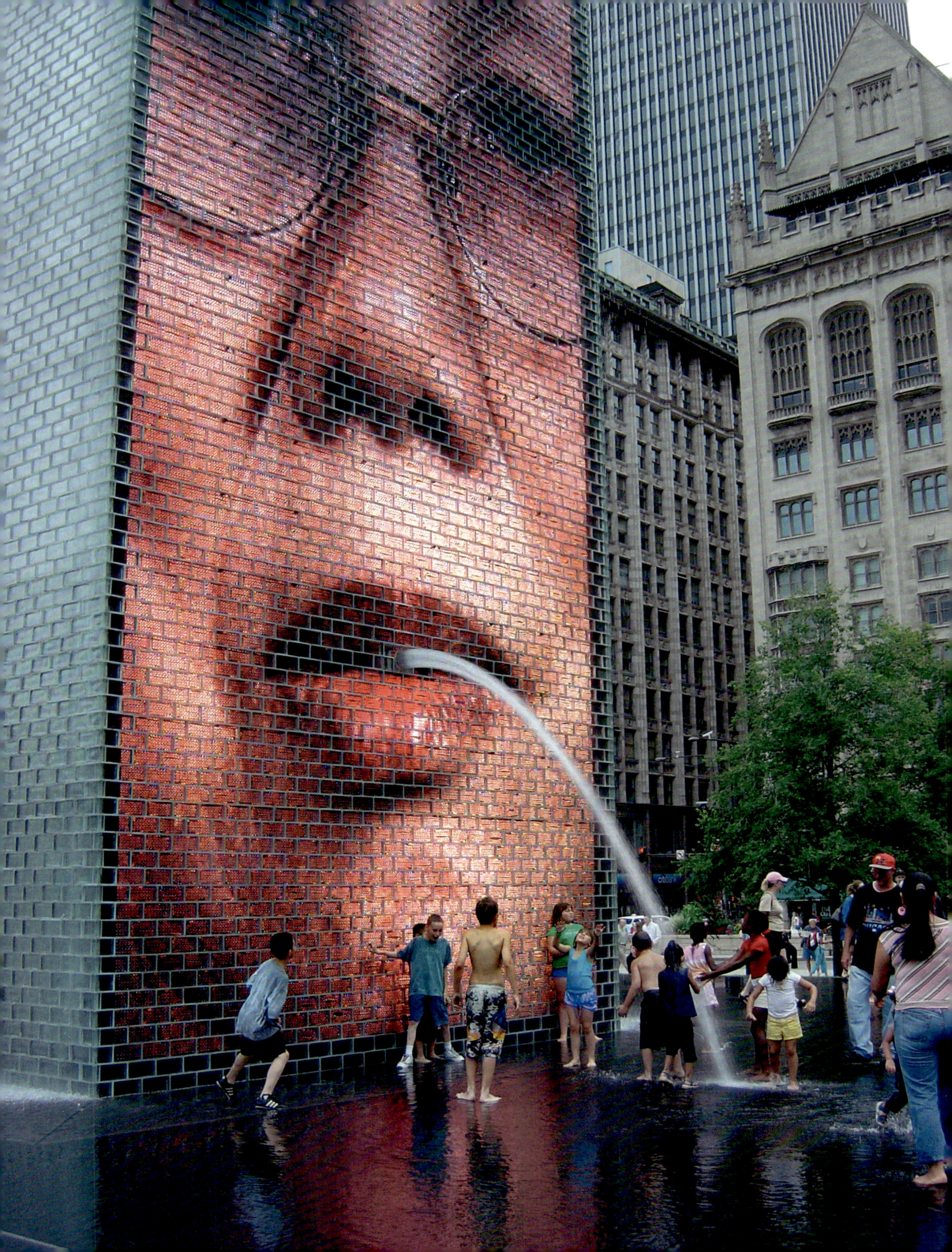

The way in which a city approaches its art in public spaces is a reflection of its goals, norms and values. Leuven is working on a future-proof vision and a holistic approach for art in public spaces. Attention is being given to revaluing the existing collection in order to make the historical images 'visible' again. Additionally, the collection will be complemented by new artworks. Today, creating and maintaining a relevant collection of art in public spaces revolves not only around artistic quality, but also around social cohesion and engaging with society. In addition to a high artistic quality, artworks are chosen on a basis of their aptitude for establishing connections, as well as making that space inclusive. This selection requires a transversal approach and a high level of collaboration between all parties concerned. It also requires a well-considered diversification of the present collection – not only in art forms (by offering, for example, a platform to other art forms, like digital arts) but also in artist profiles. By doing so, extra attention will go to gender and demographic diversity.

In line with this idea, Leuven's city administration opts for a holistic approach to art and creativity in public spaces, whereby art is not merely considered as a stand-alone object, but as an integral component of that space. "It involves [...] a way of looking at the various underlying aspects of public space. Challenging ourselves and being challenged, time and again, to research more original, more challenging, more creative, more inspiring ... alternatives."[9] One example of this approach is the close involvement of the artist duo Lola Daels and Sebastiaan Willemen in the redesign of Blauwput Square in Kessel-Lo. These artists have their say in the design discussion and are involved in all aspects of the redesign. The outcome is not any artwork in the classic sense of the word; rather, their artistic vision is being radically implemented into the final overall design.

In conclusion

Not only is our urban society a dynamic phenomenon, but also the intentions, expectations, and aesthetic parameters for art in public spaces. Important figures on pedestals share the city with artworks which invite us to touch them, to play with them or even to lie on them, such as the artwork planned by Rossella Biscotti in the Vaartkom district (2024). Ever since the very first statue was put into place (statue of Belgian statesman Sylvain Van de Weyer), Leuven has been transformed into an inclusive, livable city with residents from more than 170 different nationalities. The Hertogen site in the heart of the city is a neighborhood in full transition, which will be a crossroad for different social functions, communities, and cultural identities in the near-by future. And thus, a perfect spot for *The Four Elements* by Plensa which, by means of symbols for air, water, fire, and earth represents the different characteristics of people who together form one community.

As an age-old university town, Leuven is a cradle for reflection and critical consciousness. Its title of European Capital of Innovation (2020) recognizes this deeply-rooted tradition and motivation to use innovation as a medium for improving the quality of life of its inhabitants. In the future too, Leuven can play a main role in addressing complex societal challenges and in building a sustainable and inclusive future. From this point of view, nourishing critical reflection is essential and makes up the basis of a future-proof citizenship.

Notes

1   This tally was researched by the students of KU Leuven's Faculty of Architecture, as part of the 2022–2023 instructional lab "Atlas of Proposals," set up by the art and architecture studio Gijs Van Vaerenbergh.

2   "'de Belgen die tot de roem van hun vaderland hadden bijgedragen,'" as cited in Marika Ceunen, "(Stand)beelden in Leuven: bewegend erfgoed," in *Atlas of Proposals* (Leuven: Graphius Groep, 2023).

3   "Ze doen ons stilstaan bij het anders-zijn van het verleden, en dus ook van de toekomst." Ibid.

4   Departement CJM, "Mappingonderzoek kunst in opdracht in de publieke ruimte [research report]" (Brussels: Vlaamse Overheid. Departement Cultuur, Jeugd en Media, 2020).

5   Jacques Rancière, *The Emancipated Spectator* (New York: Verso Books, 2011).

6   Departement CJM, "Collectievorming hedendaagse kunst in de publieke ruimte: een analyse van de noden [summary report]" (Brussels: Vlaamse Overheid. Departement Cultuur, Jeugd en Media, 2022).

7   Ibid.

8   "Als je geen zorg draagt voor wat er nu al is, kan je niet verwachten dat er plots draagvlak ontstaat voor iets nieuws." Interview with Samuel Saelemaekers, in *Atlas of Proposals* (Leuven: Graphius Groep, 2023).

9   "Het gaat over (...) een manier van kijken naar de verschillende deel-aspecten van de publieke ruimte. Onszelf uitdagen en laten uitdagen om telkens originelere, uitdagendere, creatievere, meer inspirerende... alternatieven te onderzoeken." Stad Leuven, "Integrale visie publieke ruimte [final report]" (Leuven: Stad Leuven, 2023).

Literature cited

Baetens, Jan, and Lut Pil. *Kunst in de publieke ruimte.* Leuven: Leuven Univ. Press, 1998.

Boomgaard, Jeroen. *Wild Park. Het onverwachte als opdracht.* Amsterdam: Fonds voor beeldende kunsten, 2011.

Ceunen, Marika. "(Stand)beelden in Leuven: bewegend erfgoed." In *Atlas of Proposals.* Edited by Gijs Van Vaerenbergh, 6–10. Leuven: Graphius Groep, 2023.

Departement CJM. "Naar een stimulerend kunstopdrachtenbeleid voor de publieke ruimte in Vlaanderen. 8 aanbevelingen voor beleid en praktijk [research report]," edited by An Seurinck, Katrien Laenen. Brussels: Vlaamse Overheid. Departement Cultuur, Jeugd en Media, 2018.

Departement CJM. "Mappingonderzoek kunst in opdracht in de publieke ruimte [research report]," edited by Michelle Accardo, Isabelle De Voldere. Brussels: Vlaamse Overheid. Departement Cultuur, Jeugd en Media, 2020.

Departement CJM. "Collectievorming hedendaagse kunst in de publieke ruimte: een analyse van de noden [summary report]," edited by Jef Declercq, Koi Persyn. Brussels: Vlaamse Overheid. Departement Cultuur, Jeugd en Media, 2022.

Rancière, Jacques. *The Emancipated Spectator*, translated by G. Elliott. New York: Verso Books, 2011.

Roosmalen, Arno van. "Cultuur in het publieke domein, over het benutten van het maatschappelijk potentieel van kunst." Tilburg: Gemeente Tilburg, 2023.

Stad Leuven. "Integrale visie publieke ruimte [final report]." Leuven: Stad Leuven, 2023.

Vlaamse Bouwmeester. "Rond punt. Over verkeersrotondes als context voor kunst." Brussels: Mercatorfonds, 2007.

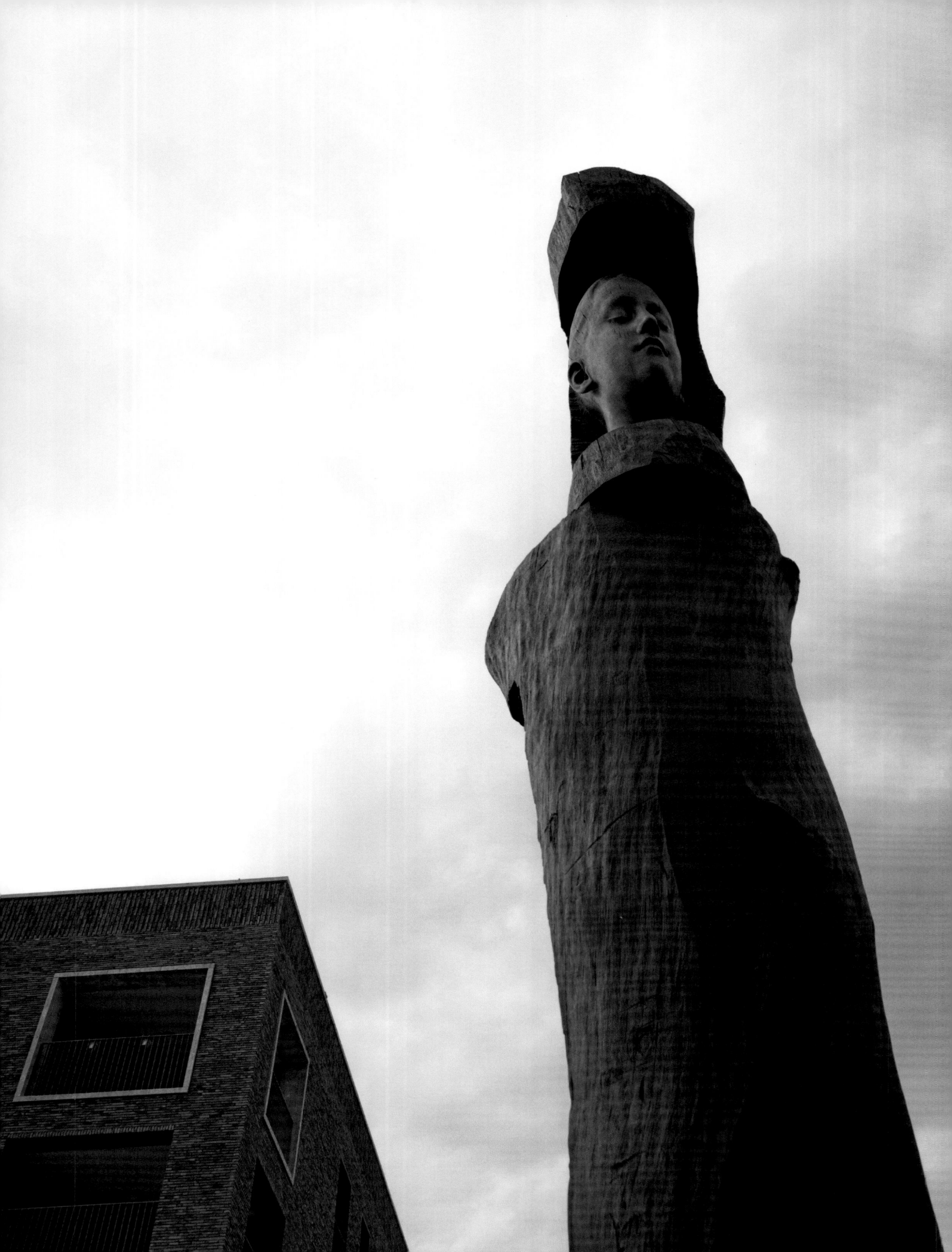

Coda
Plensa and Contemporary
KU Leuven: Four Elements,
Three Narratives, Two Locations,
One Sculpture

Geert Bouckaert

This book documents Jaume Plensa's sculpture *The Four Elements* acquired by KU Leuven. The KU Leuven *Opening the future* brain research fundraising community and its dynamic chair, Urbain Vandeurzen, took the initiative to have Plensa's sculpture in Leuven.

The Four Elements by Plensa is one sculpture consisting of two parts in bronze at two locations: the gallery of the KU Leuven University Library at Ladeuze Square and the newly created St. Raphaël's Square at the Hertogen site. This sculpture will be the first permanent work by Plensa in a Belgian public space.

The two parts of the sculpture alongside the two locations demonstrate several levels of interaction and togetherness: between the university and the city and its public spaces; between research and art; between research on health (in this case, on the brain) and organizing care. Above all, this sculpture becomes part of a trinity of images.

A Trinity of images

This sculpture is the third part of a trinity of images: the *Sedes Sapientiae*, the *Fabrica* of Vesalius, and *The Four Elements*.

The major iconographic image of KU Leuven is the *Sedes Sapientiae* ('Seat of Wisdom'). This sculpture was carved by Nicolaas De Bruyne in 1442, and is currently in the St. Peter's Church in Leuven. Plensa is in line with this *Sedes* since *The Four Elements* constitute ultimately and ideally a body of knowledge as a 'Seat of Wisdom.' The intimate face of the *Sedes* 'talks' to the intimate four faces of Plensa's sculpture.

Vesalius' publication of the *Fabrica* (1543) constitutes a major milestone in our 'knowledge of the body' impacting medical sciences, as well as the arts of representing, imaging, and imagining bodies. Vesalius wanted to know the elements of the body by 'unpacking' the body in its components. Plensa's *The Four Elements* also looks at the 'knowledge of the body,' showing the fragility of our vulnerable bodies.

The Four Elements consists of symbols representing fire, earth, water, and air to create a human form, while also signifying the different characteristics that bring people together to shape a humanity. It also demonstrates the fragility of humans as individuals and of humans in societies on planet Earth. These four elements only make sense when you bring them together and when a synergy of elements is created. Connecting the diversity of elements creates meaning for an individual, as well as for society. The four faces have a diversity of ethnicity which shows that plurality is needed in society.

Plensa and his *Four Elements* finalize a triptych on the 'body of knowledge' with a triptych on the 'knowledge of body'. The 'Seats of Wisdom' now consist of De Bruyne's 1442 *Sedes Sapientiae*, Vesalius's 1543 *Fabrica*, and Plensa's 2024 *Four Elements*.

Linking KU Leuven and the City of Leuven:
Research and care for the brain, health, and memory

This sculpture shows many points of connection between KU Leuven and the City of Leuven. The historically developed homeostasis of public and semi-public spaces in Leuven shows the nature of KU Leuven and the City of Leuven as conjoined twins. Plensa's sculpture underscores this linkage by having *The Four Elements* together in two locations watching one another.

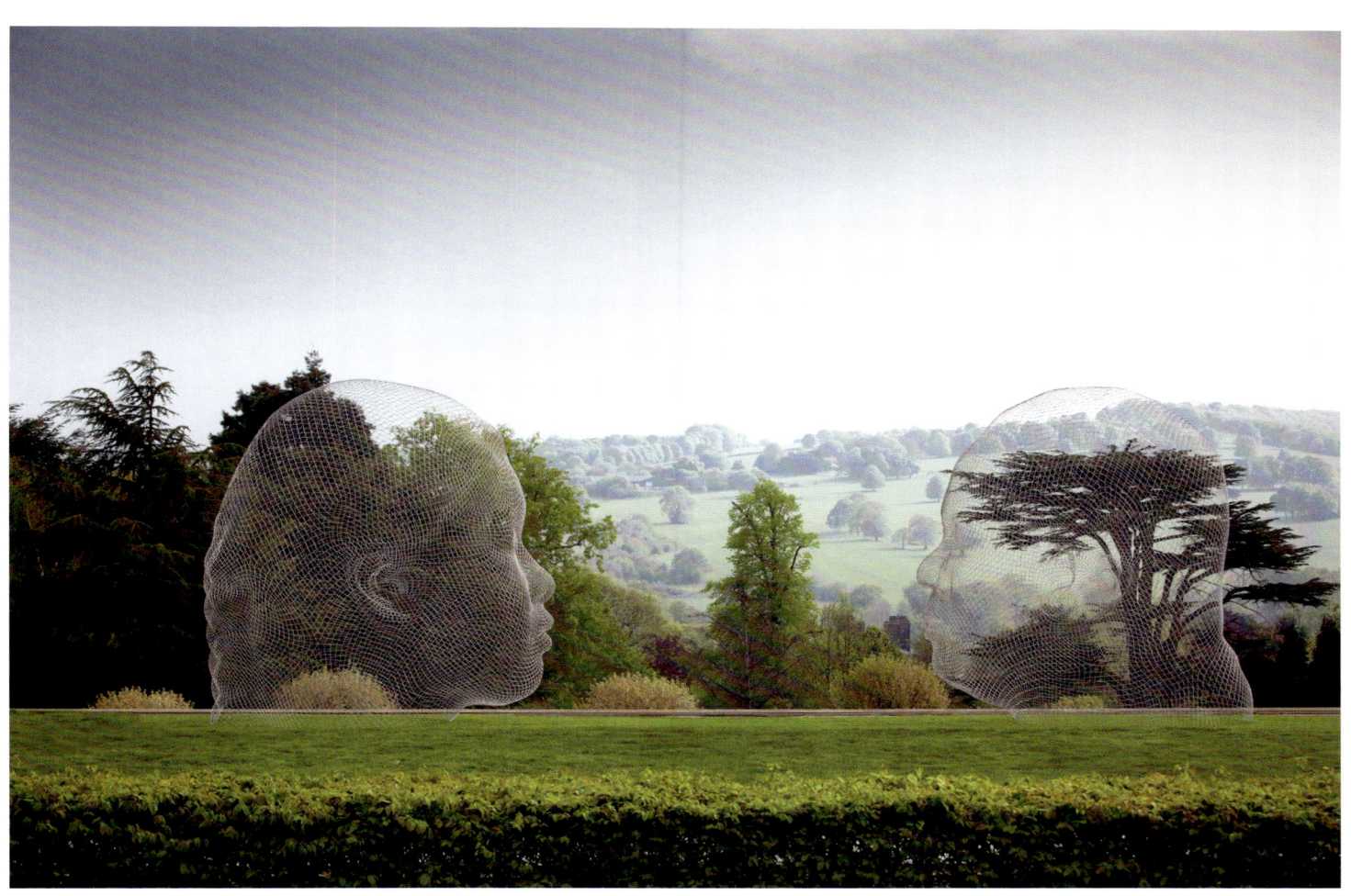

It is not a coincidence that the two locations of Plensa's sculpture are the University Library as a seat of wisdom, and St. Raphaël's Square as a central crossroads of health highways watching Gasthuisberg, the new Vesalius Museum, and the Hertogen site, which has a history of hospitality within the City of Leuven for taking care of people.

The University Library is an obvious historical location, especially for the 'fire' element of the four elements. It is also an explicit reference to the fragility of a library as a seat of wisdom and societal memory. St. Raphaël's Square also is an obvious historical location on a site that is still full of references to medical research institutions, not to mention hospitals taking care of fragile bodies. The elements of water, earth, and air are at this crossroads, as a totem, watching in different directions old and current hospitals (Gasthuisberg) alongside the Vesalius Museum site with its historical anatomic theater.

A Janus-faced vision for a contemporary university: Science and art

When there is a disintegration and disconnection of the elements constituting our body and certainly our brains, and even our societies, we suffer from memory loss as an individual and also as a society. Our scientific research tries to disentangle the mysteries of our bodies and the functioning of our societies. De Bruyn, Vesalius, and Plensa try to image and imagine these mysteries.

The *Sedes*, *Fabrica*, and *Four Elements* are all at the crossroads of looking at reality in a Janus-faced manner. Universities need 'wisdom' to understand complex realities. This requires scientific as well as artistic research, which needs to impact teaching and service to our societies.

A contemporary university focuses on contemporaneity, which means that our current scientific and artistic research will be relevant for the future. Universities need 'wisdom' to create spaces for creativity, innovation, experiments, and new languages, all of which allow us to image and imagine our bodies, our societies, and our worlds. The *Sedes Sapientiae*, the *Fabrica*, and *The Four Elements* are essential artistic expressions of how to image and imagine our remaining mysteries.

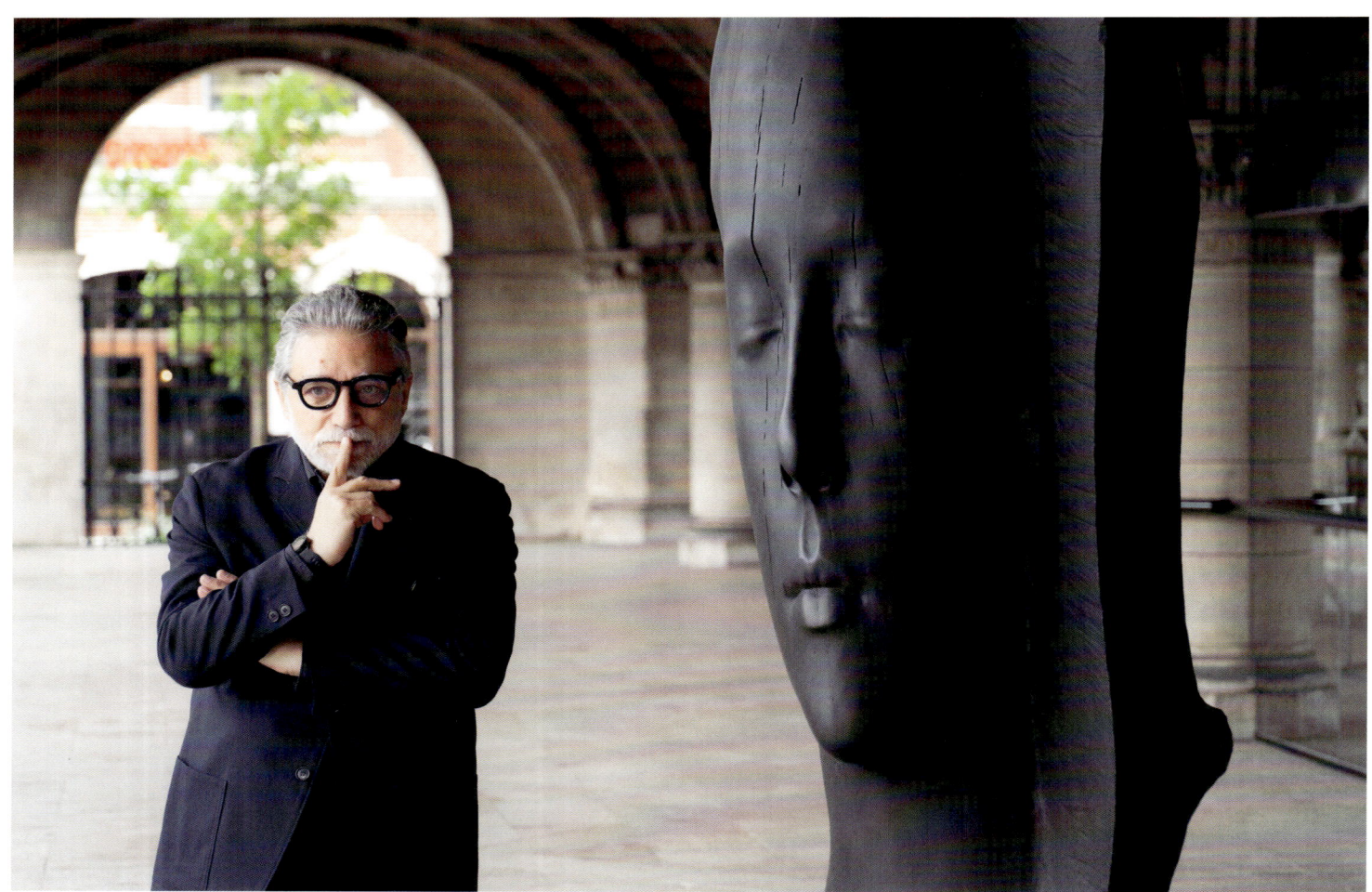

Jaume Plensa and *The Four Elements – Fire.* © Michaël de Lausnay

Biography Jaume Plensa

Jaume Plensa creates sculptures and installations that unite individuals through connections of spirituality, the body, and collective memory. Literature, psychology, biology, language, and history have been key guiding elements throughout his career. Using a wide range of materials including steel, cast iron, resin, paraffin wax, glass, light, water, and sound, Plensa lends physical weight and volume to components of the human and the ephemeral conditions.

Plensa is highly active in projects in public space: his celebrated works can be seen at Bonaventure Gateway, Montreal; Millennium Park, Chicago; Olympic Sculpture Park, Seattle; Burj Khalifa, Dubai; BBC Broadcasting Tower, London, and St. Helens, Liverpool; Pearson International Airport, Toronto; Daikanyama and Toranomon Hills, Tokyo; Ogijima, Takamatsu; MIT, Boston; Albright Knox Art Gallery, Buffalo; Rice University, Houston; Bastion Saint-Jaume, Antibes; Pérez Art Museum, Miami, among many other sites worldwide. The artist has presented solo exhibitions at prestigious institutions around the globe, most recently in 2022 at the Museum Oscar Niemeyer, Curitiba, Brazil; the MACBA–Museu d'Art Contemporani de Barcelona, Spain, which travelled to the Moscow Museum of Modern Art, Russia in 2019; and at Museo Nacional Centro de Arte Reina Sofía, Madrid in 2018. Other solo museum exhibitions include Musée d'art moderne et contemporain de Saint-Étienne, France; Nasher Sculpture Center, Dallas, Texas; Musée Picasso, Antibes, France; Yorkshire Sculpture Park, England; and the Espoo Museum of Modern Art, Finland.

Jaume Plensa: Together was presented at the Basilica San Giorgio Maggiore in Italy as a collateral event of the 56th Venice Biennale (2015). The artist was honored for the Best International Public Outdoor Installation, at the Miami Dade College, and also at the Hirshhorn New York Gala in 2019. He received the Honor of Chevalier des Arts et Lettres in France 1993 and the Velázquez Award for Art in Madrid 2013, among other accolades.

The artist was born in Barcelona, Spain in 1955, where he currently lives and works.

Selected Artworks
Jaume Plensa

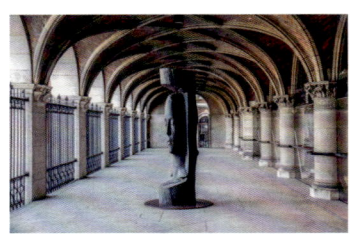

cover
The Four Elements – Fire, 2024.
Leuven.
© Rob Stevens

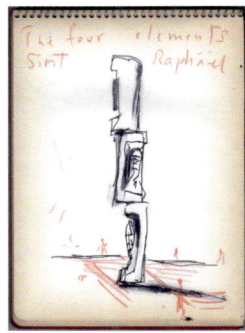

p. 6
The Four Elements, 2024. Sketch.
© Plensa Studio Barcelona

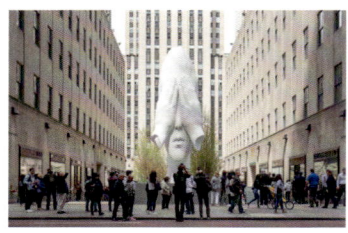

p. 10
Behind the Walls, 2018.
Rockefeller Center, New York, USA.
Photo Timothy Schenck © Frieze Sculpture

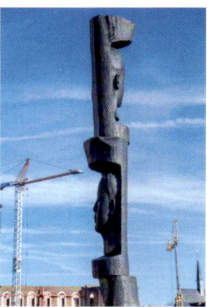

p. 14
The Four Elements – Earth, Air, 2024.
Leuven.
© Rob Stevens

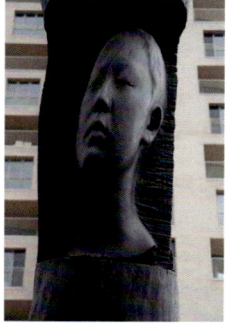

p. 22
The Four Elements – Earth, 2024.
Leuven.
© Michaël de Lausnay

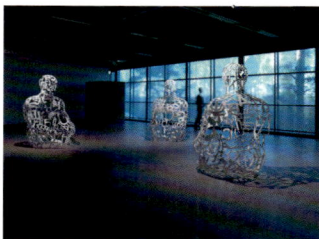

p. 28
The Three Graces I, II, and III, 2010.
EMMA – Espoo Museum of Modern Art, Helsinki, Finland.
Photo Ari Karttunen © EMMA

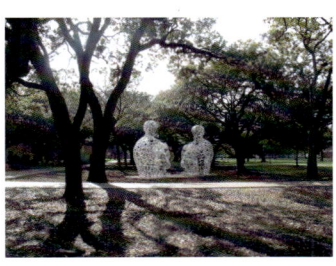

p. 29
Mirror, 2011.
Rice University, Houston, USA.
Photo Laura Medina © Plensa Studio Barcelona

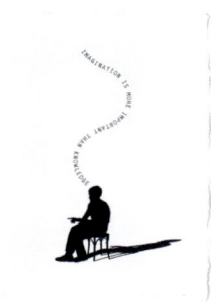

p. 31
Les Silhouettes I, 2012. Etching.
Photo Gasull Fotografia © Plensa Studio Barcelona

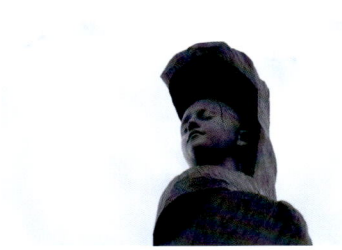

p. 36
The Four Elements – Air, 2024.
Leuven.
© Michaël de Lausnay

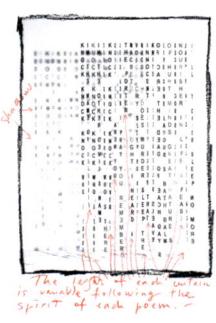

p. 64
Twentynine Palms, 2007. Sketch.
© Plensa Studio Barcelona

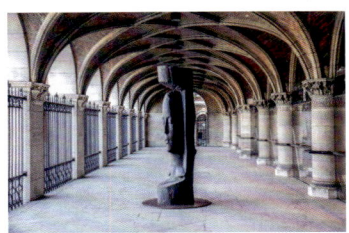

p. 68
The Four Elements – Fire, 2024.
Leuven.
© Rob Stevens

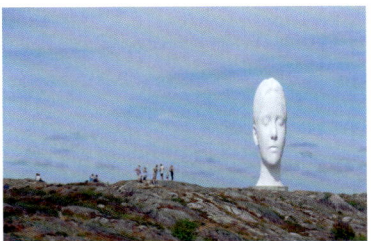

p. 71
Anna, 2015.
Pilane Heritage Museum, Sweden.
Photo Peter Lennby © Pilane Heritage Museum

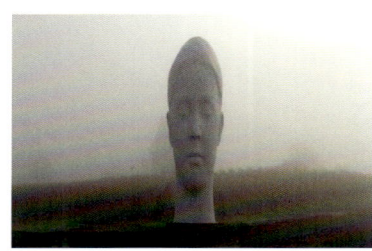

p. 72
Sanna, 2016.
The Donum Estate, USA.
Photo Anthony Laurino © The Donum Estate

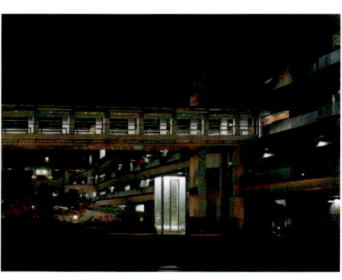

p. 75
Transparant Doubts, 2000.
University of Shizuoka for Culture and Art, Hamamatsu, Japan.
Photo by Yosuke Tsuzuki © Plensa Studio Barcelona

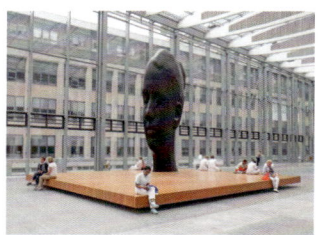

p. 76
Duna, 2014.
Erasmus Medical Centre, Rotterdam, The Netherlands.
© Erasmus MC

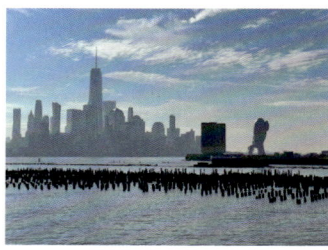

p. 81
Water's Soul, 2020.
Newport, Jersey City, USA.
Photo Timothy Schenck © Plensa Studio Barcelona

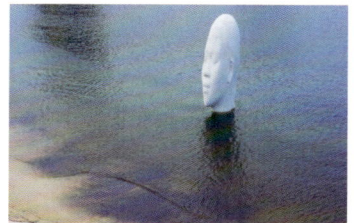

p. 93
Awilda, Olhar Nos Meus Sonhos, 2012.
Rio de Janeiro, Brazil.
© Marcello Dantas

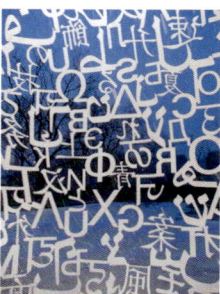

p. 96
Detail from *Body of Knowledge*, 2010.
Goethe-Universität, Frankfurt, Germany.
Photo Laura Medina © Plensa Studio Barcelona

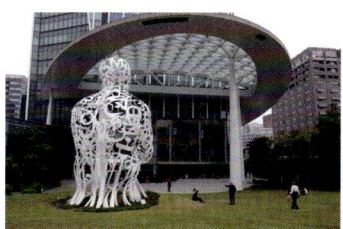

p. 100
Roots, 2014.
Mori Building, Tokyo, Japan.
Photo Laura Medina © Plensa Studio Barcelona

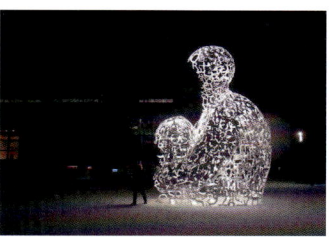

p. 103
Body of Knowledge, 2010.
Goethe-Universität, Frankfurt, Germany.
Photo Laura Medina © Plensa Studio Barcelona

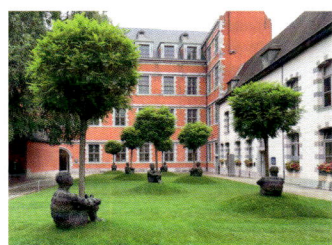

p. 105
The Heart of Trees.
Installation view of "La Part du Sacré".
Jardin du Mayeur, 2023. Mons, Belgium.
Photo Laura Medina © Plensa Studio Barcelona

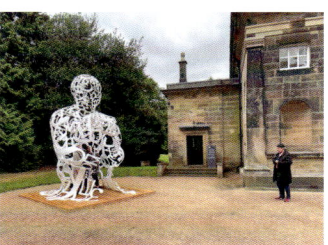

p. 106
White Nomad, 2021.
Yorkshire Sculpture Park, West Bretton, UK.
© Plensa Studio Barcelona

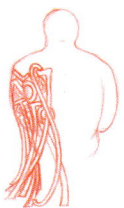

p. 109
Roots. Sketch.
© Plensa Studio Barcelona

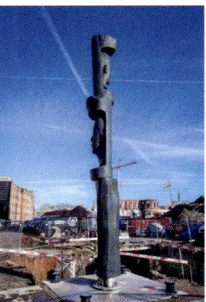

p. 115
The Four Elements – Water, Earth, Air, 2024.
Leuven.
© Rob Stevens

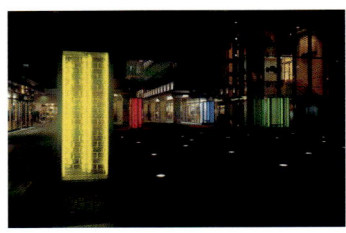

p. 125
Seven Deities of Good Fortune, 2000.
Daikanyama, Shibuya, Tokyo, Japan.
Photo © ANAZ ï

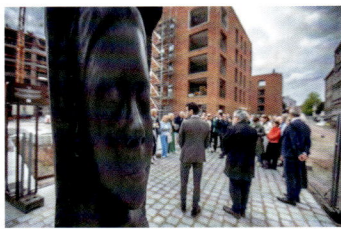

p. 128
The Four Elements – Water, 2024.
Leuven.
© Rob Stevens

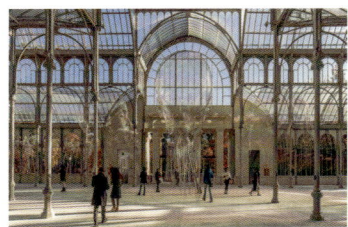

p. 131
Invisibles, 2018.
Museo Nacional Centro de Arte Reina Sofia, Madrid, Spain.
Photo Luís Asín © Plensa Studio Barcelona

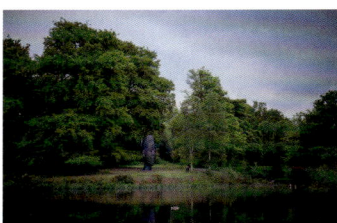

p. 135
Wilsis, 2016.
Yorkshire Sculpture Park, UK.
Photo Jonty Wilde © Yorkshire Sculpture Park

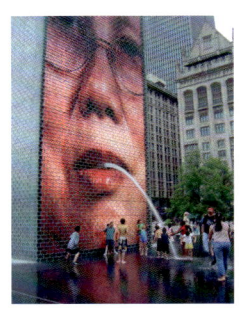

p. 136
The Crown Fountain, 2004.
Milennium Park, Chicago, USA.
Photo Laura Medina © Plensa studio Barcelona

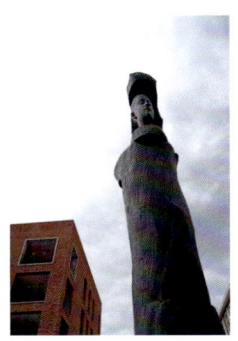

p. 140
The Four Elements – Air, 2024.
Leuven.
© Michaël de Lausnay

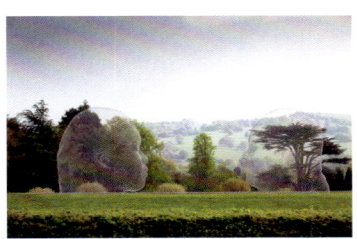

p. 143
Nuria 2007, and *Irma*, 2010.
Yorkshire Sculpture Park, West Bretton, UK.
Photo Jonty Wilde © Yorkshire Sculpture Park

About the Authors

GEERT BOUCKAERT is a professor emeritus at the Public Governance Institute, KU Leuven. He is the chair of the KU Leuven Commission for Contemporary Art and the president of Leuven University Press.

MARK DEREZ is the former archivist for KU Leuven.

REBECCA GYSEN is the head of the Heritage and Archives Department for the City of Leuven.

STÉFANIE LAMBRECHTS is a cultural policy advisor in the Culture Division for the City of Leuven. She is also affiliated with LUCA School of Arts, KU Leuven.

KAREN LANDUYDT is the City of Leuven's development coordinator for its *benedenstad* ('downtown') district.

STÉPHANE SYMONS is a professor at the Institute of Philosophy, KU Leuven, at its Center for Metaphysics, Philosophy of Culture; he is a member of the KU Leuven Commission for Contemporary Art.

ERIK THYS is a psychiatrist at the University Psychiatric Center, Z.Org and KU Leuven, as well as a professor at LUCA School of Arts, KU Leuven.

TOM VAN IMSCHOOT teaches literature, art writing, essayism and critical reflection on the arts at LUCA School of Arts. He leads the Image Research Unit for Sint-Lucas Visual Arts in Ghent, and is also extraordinary visiting professor in the arts at the Associated Faculty of Arts, KU Leuven.

JOHAN WAGEMANS is a professor at KU Leuven's Faculty of Psychology and Educational Sciences, at its Brain and Cognition Research Unit.

Colophon

Acknowledgements

This book project could only be realized with the substantial support of the Stichting Amici Almae Matris and its chair, Professor Filip Abraham, along with the encouragement and support of Professor Koen Debackere, president of the KU Leuven Association.

Special thanks, too, to Wim Desmet, KU Leuven Managing Director, Stefaan Saeys and Joris Snaet with their team of our KU Leuven Technical Services Department, and Anne Verbrugge, Head of Art Heritage, for their professional support, as well as the whole team of Leuven University Press, under the leadership of director Nienke Roelants.

The editor also wants to recognize the unconditional support of Galeria Senda in Barcelona, with Carlos Duran.

This book would not have been possible without the generous support and contributions of Studio Plensa in Barcelona, especially Jaume Plensa and Laura Plensa.

Publication

Editorial direction: Geert Bouckaert in collaboration with Nienke Roelants

Translation and copy-editing: John R. Eyck

Graphic Design: Theo van Beurden Studio

Published in 2024 by Leuven University Press / Presses Universitaires de Louvain / Universitaire Pers Leuven. Minderbroedersstraat 4, B-3000 Leuven (Belgium).

Selection and editorial matter © 2024, Geert Bouckaert

Individual chapters © 2024, The respective authors

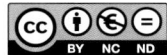
ISBN 978 94 6270 432 9 (hardcover)
eISBN 978 94 6166 600 0 (ePDF)
eISBN 978 94 6166 601 7 (ePuB)
https://doi.org/10.11116/9789461666000
D/2024/1869/37
NUR: 646